# Living with Autistic Spectrum Disorders

## Guidance for Parents, Carers and Siblings

Elizabeth Attfield and
Hugh Morgan

P·C·P

Paul Chapman
Publishing

Paul Chapman Publishing
A SAGE Publications Company
1 Oliver's Yard
55 City Road
London EC1Y 1SP

SAGE Publications Inc
2455 Teller Road
Thousand Oaks, California 91320

SAGE Publications India Pvt Ltd
B-42, Panchsheel Enclave
Post Box 4109
New Delhi 110 017

**Library of Congress Control Number 2006931453**

A catalogue record for this book is available
from the British Library

ISBN 10: 1-4129-2328-X          ISBN 13: 978 1-4129-2328-6
ISBN 10: 1-4129-2329-8          ISBN 13: 978 1-4129-2329-3 (pbk)

Typeset by C&M Digitals (P) Ltd., Chennai, India
Printed in Great Britain by Athenaeum Press Ltd, Gateshead, Tyne & Wear
Printed on paper from sustainable resources

# Living with Autistic Spectrum Disorders

# Contents

# About the authors

## Elizabeth Attfield

Elizabeth Attfield is a Training Officer for autism.west midlands www.autism westmidlands.org.uk, with a specific remit for developing family training and co-ordinating accredited autism training for teaching staff. She has worked for this regional charity for the past seven years but also has a wealth of professional and personal experience to draw upon. After initially working as a secondary school teacher she then retrained as a primary school teacher and worked in both mainstream and specialist settings across the age and ability range before becoming a Parent Partnership Officer. Elizabeth has a son with autism who recently, at the age of 19 years, made the transition to specialist adult provision. Together with her husband Ian, Elizabeth delivers workshops and seminars on the joys and challenges of parenting a child with autism.

## Hugh Morgan

Hugh Morgan has been Chief Executive of Autism Cymru, Wales' national charity for autism, since 2001. He had previously worked as the lead officer for the West Midlands Autistic Society (now autism.west midlands) for 14 years. Hugh started working in the learning disabilities and autism field back in 1975 and has worked in a variety of hands-on settings with children and especially adults with autism. Hugh played a key role in the development of the autism training courses established by the University of Birmingham since 1990; and in 2003/4 was chair of the External Working Group for the autism strategy being developed by the National Assembly for Wales. Hugh is co-founder and editor of the *Good Autism Practice Journal* and an associate editor of *Autism* published by Sage/NAS. Hugh has professional and academic qualifications in psychology, social work, medical science and originally in nursing.

# Acknowledgements

Our appreciation goes to Ian Attfield for reading and commenting upon the draft of this book, to Terry Weston for his helpful comments, and to those many excellent people we have both worked with over many years in autism.west midlands and Autism Cymru and elsewhere, who have shaped our conceptual thinking and practice. Finally, we pay a big debt to individuals with autism and their families, without whom this book would not have been possible.

# How to use this book

This book is one of a series and is aimed at parents, carers and other family members who are living with autistic spectrum disorders and are looking for information in coming to terms with the reality of this and some ideas for accessing support. The focus of the book is upon children and adolescents with autistic spectrum disorders (ASD) and their families rather than upon adults and older people with ASD. This latter group deserves recognition in a further book dedicated to their needs.

*Living with Autistic Spectrum Disorders* addresses the emotional issues that are thrown up when a child in the family has autism and offers some practical strategies to help families cope. It also aims to provide useful sources of information for accessing services and support and working through the 'system' – for example, to choose a school or manage the move into adult services. Families can dip into the chapters that meet their needs at the time and come back to further sections as circumstances change and they reach the next stage in their child's life. While acknowledging the devastating impact that autism in the family can have on everyday life, the emphasis is on drawing out the positives and concentrating on how to make living with autism a better experience, rather than dwelling solely on the negatives. The terms 'autism' and 'autistic spectrum disorders' are used in an interchangeable way for stylistic ease rather than signifying a difference between the two. 'He' has been used throughout the book rather than alternating between 'he' and 'she' to reflect the fact that more boys than girls are affected by autism.

*Note:* In England, education, health and social services are having to change the way they work, in line with the aims of government policy of

'Every Child Matters' so local authorities are merging individual services under the umbrella of 'Children's Services' and changing their policies and procedures. The difficulty in England is that at the point of writing this book the terminology we have all been used to is to change. As this is all so new, we have decided to stick with familiar terms such as Local Education Authority (LEA), even though LEAs are already going out of existence in some areas, rather than confuse readers with new jargon they are not yet accustomed to. In Wales, Scotland and Northern Ireland, where political devolution has led to self-determination in terms of education and health policy, the impact of changes in English policy is less apparent but equally the opportunities presented by each nation's own education policies are evolving.

# Understanding the parental emotional rollercoaster

This chapter looks at the rollercoaster impact of the diagnosis of autistic spectrum disorder upon parents, where expectations change over time, but how encouragement can be gained from apparent adversity.

## Living in a social world

The family with autism live in a wider social world. It may seem unfair that this wider population will hold a variety of perceptions about autism ranging from ignorance through a gamut of myths, legends, falsehoods and just occasionally empathy and understanding.

Both authors have spoken to parents over the past 20 years and it is obvious that for many families life with autism can be a lifelong struggle. The family with autism has to make its way in the social world from the time the child with autism is born. For parents particularly, life circumstances can seem extremely daunting and often feelings of isolation and the need to fight tooth and nail to push forward the need for services for their son or daughter become the prime motivators of family life.

Today we are moving into an era where, just possibly, the cause of families with autism is being listened to and felt more by governments and the planners of educational and care services, and therefore more support may be made available than ever before.

Perhaps this is a bold statement to make but there is clear evidence in support of this view, as in recent years we have seen significant developments in each of the UK's countries. It may be helpful to recap very briefly on political developments in the field of autism.

In Wales, following substantial lobbying work of ministers by Autism Cymru, the Welsh Assembly Government have been developing a ten-year national strategy for autistic spectrum disorders which, according to Wales' ministers, is due to start in 2007/8 (Henwood, 2003).

Likewise, the considerable lobbying work in Northern Ireland (NI) by Autism Northern Ireland (PAPA) is leading to consideration by the Northern Ireland Assembly of the development of a Northern Ireland Autism Act (Coulter, 2006). This NI charity is also campaigning hard for a NI Assembly-led national strategy for autism.

In Scotland, the Scottish Executive have produced very good working reports on autism, especially *The Public Health Institute Autistic Spectrum Disorder Needs Assessment Report* (Scottish Executive, 2001), and the Scottish Society for Autism is lobbying for the development of a national autism strategy in Scotland.

In England, although there has been no ownership to date by Westminster in the development of a formal national ASD strategy nor indeed any attempt to move forward with primary legislation for autism, the manifesto of APPGA (All Party Parliamentary Group for Autism) sets out the rights of people with autism. In addition, several influential reports have been produced, e.g. *Guidelines for Good Practice* (DfES, 2002); the *National Autism Plan for Children* (NAP-C) (NAS, 2003) and *Psychiatric Services for Adolescents and Adults with Asperger Syndrome and Other Autistic Spectrum Disorders* (Royal College of Psychiatrists, 2006).

Ten years ago, none of this movement at strategic levels existed within the field of autism, so it can been seen that considerable progress has been made by a whole range of large and small voluntary organisations and public agencies alike in inspiring and helping to achieve significant steps forward, based upon foundations laid by the heroic work of parents and practitioners over previous decades. The cautionary note, however, is that the impact of these great strides can only be determined by the way in which they lead to improvements in the quality of life for individuals and their families, and there is a need for serious research to evaluate this effect.

## Changing expectations: the parental grief cycle

As parents we do not plan to have a child with autism. Rather, we anticipate having children who, as they grow older, will themselves become self-sufficient and independent, and experience the desire to have their own children, in the same way that we have.

Parents experience a mix of emotions when they are told their child has a disability – especially when that disability is a hidden one, like autism. Parents find that they may have been lulled into a false sense of security regarding their child's development up to that point and now it's a 'double whammy' to find that the perfect child they thought they had does not exist and they must adjust their aspirations and expectations accordingly.

For some parents, who knew instinctively that 'something was not right', there may be relief at getting a diagnosis and being able to put a name to the difficulties they and their child are experiencing. They then discover they can do something about it by finding out about the condition and seeking information and interventions to help them deal with it. This then becomes a coping strategy as much as the temporary withdrawal from the world that other parents employ.

Coming to terms with the reality of what the diagnosis may mean for the family is a grief cycle akin to bereavement and parents need plenty of time and tolerance from others as they move from one stage to another. There is likely to be tremendous shock and denial.

'It can't be true! It's not fair ... why him? ... why us?' The sense of injustice, the anger, guilt and feelings of powerlessness and despair, may overwhelm parents before they finally come to accept their child for who s/he is.

Parents need to know that it is not their fault that their child has an autistic spectrum disorder and learn not to blame themselves for a quirk of fate. They need to give themselves permission to grieve, not to feel they have to 'put on a brave face' all the time and pretend they are not devastated by the realisation that their world will never be the same again and their lives will be altered in unimaginable ways. *It is OK to cry!*

It's a tough time emotionally and nobody from outside the family can really help parents through it. But, as they begin to appreciate their child's unique personality and see some of the positives of having a child who is different – and this may take years – some of the hurt will go away, but never completely, because you still feel the loss of the child you wanted, planned for, and thought you had.

## Understanding the emotional rollercoaster

| Natural responses of parenthood | Disability in the family |
|---|---|
| Unconditional love | Unconditional love tempered by sadness |
| Bonding | Bonding process damaged |
| Reciprocity<br>• Emotion<br>• Response<br>• Interaction | May be no reciprocity |
| Protectiveness | (Over)protectiveness |
| Positive emotions associated with child's development and progress from childhood to adulthood:<br>• Joy<br>• Pleasure<br>• Pride<br>• Excitement<br>• Fun | Negative emotions associated with child's development and possible lack of progress:<br>• Sense of loss<br>• Grief<br>• Fear<br>• Anxiety<br>• Worry |
| High expectations | Lower expectations |
| High aspirations | Lower aspirations |
| Future plans | Concerns for the future |
| Growing confidence in own parenting skills | Lack of confidence in own parenting skills |
| Diminishing responsibility as young person takes on more responsibility for self | Overwhelming responsibility: young person lacks ability to take on responsibility for self |
| Sense of achievement in part played in child's upbringing and development | Less sense of achievement because child's development is 'different' |
| Feeling of belonging | Isolation |
| Inclusion | Exclusion |

## Parents – the pioneers of the autism movement

An important early point for parents of the newly diagnosed child with autism to realise is that they are not alone. They are by absolute right 'members' of a very large movement in the United Kingdom and wherever they should live in the UK there are likely to be other families with autism not very far from them. Quite possibly there will be a local support group that they can join, and indeed other parents that they can talk to who have been or are going through similar experiences.

History speaks for the strength of families with autism and of the successes they have made in moving forward the cause of autism in the world today. It is parents who have played the key role in the development of public awareness and in the development of services for people with autism. During the critical early years of the 1960s, 1970s and 1980s when autism was a condition recognised by very few members of the public (and indeed the medical and social care professions), it was the drive and initiative of parents who almost single-handedly moved forward the development of services for both children and adults with autism. These parents, who started several powerful autistic charities in key geographical areas, should be viewed today as the pioneers of the autism movement.

### Points to remember

- Experiencing a variety of emotions is perfectly natural for parents
- Expectations are likely to change over time
- Parents need not feel alone; many have trodden the path before

# 2

# Brothers and sisters and wider family issues

This chapter looks at the perspective of brothers and sisters of children with autism, with particular emphasis upon the adolescent siblings whose own maturational changes and peer group pressures bring their own challenges. It also considers wider issues where there is autism in the family.

## The younger sibling

There has been a growth of interest in recent years in the siblings of children with autism. The recognition of the important part that siblings play in the life of the child with autism, their own needs, desires and position in the family structure, in addition to their own adjustment to autism in the family, is somewhat overdue.

There are a number of books aimed at younger siblings such as *Children with Autism: A Booklet for Brothers and Sisters* (Davies, 1995b); the equivalent for the siblings of children with Asperger syndrome by the same author (1995a); and also the recent award-winning bilingual (Welsh/English) booklet *My Brother Gwern* (Walker-Jones, 2005), which are all well received by families and in the case of the latter can be obtained free of charge from Autism Cymru. Other useful books in this field are *My Brother is Different* (Gorrod, 1997) and *Everybody is Different* (Bleach, 2001).

In the younger age group the focus of the literature has been to help the sibling to recognise and understand why their brother or sister is different.

These booklets are about saying 'it is OK' and indeed to be proud of the brother or sister with autism and of their idiosyncratic interests, while at the same time acknowledging that it is also perfectly admissible to moan about the sibling with autism and to find him/her 'a pain'. Conflict between siblings is natural and siblings of children with autism need not feel guilty for not always appreciating the foibles of their brother or sister.

For the older sibling though, publications either on the web or indeed in book form are very hard to find. Yet, as the child with autism gets older, so do their siblings, and so the impact of autism upon the sibling changes and can have unforeseen implications.

## The adolescent sibling

For the adolescent brother or sister of the person with autism some pretty strong feelings may kick in, motivated primarily by an embarrassment factor, and there may be negative and even angry feelings against the child who spoils games, destroys possessions, makes a noise and a mess and causes disruption. There may also be a feeling that family life and social life are becoming constrained, restricted and disrupted. Siblings may be embarrassed about what to tell their friends when they come home and may choose not to bring friends home – with particular concerns at the time of the first girlfriend or boyfriend. Additionally, siblings may feel they have to compete for parental attention and are 'second best' because so much time and energy have to be directed to a child with a disability, and they may come to resent this. A healthy expression in the family home by the brother or sister of humour and non-politically correct terminology when referring to the sibling with autism, and even rebelling against professionals and family, may be of help.

Brothers or sisters are likely to experience confusing and conflicting emotions. They may also defend their ASD sibling to the hilt to others and have considerable pride in their achievements; interestingly they often find themselves in turn idolised by their ASD sibling. As a result they are likely to experience a sense of guilt at feeling negative or hostile emotions, culminating in frustration and possible aggression or withdrawal, great sadness and regret that there is this disability to live with. Possibly their own behaviour may deteriorate as an attention-seeking strategy, causing parents further stress, or they may worry about parents not coping and the family splitting up, especially if there is a lot of family disharmony.

The brother or sister may feel the burden of having to be good at everything to compensate for the sibling with autism's deficits, or may rebel at such perceived expectations from parents. Indeed, parents need to be aware of placing a large burden of carrying parental hopes for the future as 'the successful one'. Parents also need to be aware that the young carer may grow up too soon and may resent the loss of a carefree childhood or secretly harbour concerns they do not wish to voice with regard to the likelihood that they also might have a child with ASD when they come to have a family of their own. These are real concerns that need acknowledging and addressing. For more information about support for siblings, see the final chapter of this book.

## Decision-making within the family

All brothers and sisters and parents will have worries about the future – who will be responsible when parents die? Individual siblings will be largely on their own, whereas in families where there are two or more siblings the potential for shared arrangements will be an advantage.

One of the problems of putting systems in place, like discretionary trusts, to minimise future worries and ensure financial security for the person with autism, is that there is inconsistency in legal advice and changes in legislation do take place, so families need to find a solicitor well versed in SEN legislation around making wills and setting up trust funds. Mencap produce some useful guidelines that may be of assistance.

---

### How to help siblings

- Opportunities to meet other siblings and share experiences
- Being kept informed and involved in decisions about sibling
- 'Special time' with parents away from sibling
- Feeling valued for own sake
- Forward planning for the future so burden of responsibility is reduced
- Circles of support for family
- Acknowledgement of unique sibling experience and ongoing role in disabled person's life
- Time and opportunity to have fun and live own life, without guilt
- Acceptance that it is OK to express dissatisfaction with sibling

---

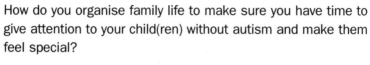

**REFLECTIVE OASIS**

How do you show all the children in your family that they are valued for their own sakes?

How do you organise family life to make sure you have time to give attention to your child(ren) without autism and make them feel special?

How do you acknowledge the role, feelings and worries of the brother(s) and sister(s) of your child with autism and involve them in future planning and the present life of their sibling?

## Wider family issues

Families come in all kinds of shapes and sizes and we need to take on board the principle of the 'self-defining family', a phrase coined by Carpenter (2000). He points out that the concept of the traditional nuclear family is outmoded – many children now grow up in single parent families, or in 'second' families with step-parents and step-brothers and sisters. Some are raised by grandparents, others by relatives or in extended families, and others are cared for by adoptive parents or foster-carers.

With such diversity comes a need to look at the concerns of the whole family involved in the life of the child with the disability – and let's not forget the neighbours, family friends and 'significant others' in the child's life, whose role may be crucial to the support and well-being of the family of the child with autism. They all have an important perspective that must be taken into account, and family dynamics will be very much affected by their responses and attitudes to the child with autism and the amount of support, both practical and emotional, they are able to offer the child's parents.

The role of grandparents, in particular, must be recognised. For grandparents it may be doubly difficult to come to terms with the idea of autism in the family because they are worried not only about the welfare of their grandchild, but also the stress on their adult son/daughter of having a child with autism. Yet, either or both grandparents can provide extremely valuable support to the family with autism. Grandparents may often take a very pragmatic approach to autism in the family; after all, they have already brought up their own children and have knowledge and 'wisdom' not often displayed by younger parents. Grandparents are good seekers and sifters of information on autism, which can be passed on to the parents, who should then expect to make their own decisions with total support from the grandparents. Grandparents can be great emotional props for their son or daughter bringing up a child with autism and can provide both moral and practical support and guidance in a crisis.

Ethnic, cultural and religious attitudes also come into play here. In some cultures, any disability brings stigma along with it. The need of minority ethnic families in terms of understanding, tolerance and support services is certainly no less than within the wider population and, in terms of specific support services for ethnic minority families, there is indeed a dramatic lack of workers skilled in autism who speak Asian or African languages (Corea, 2003). A campaign has been led by Ivan Corea to increase the voice of people with autistic spectrum disorders and their families as a way of obtaining better services (for example, visit **http://autism-ethnic-uk.tripod.com**).

### Points to remember

- Siblings of all ages need to understand how autism affects their brother/sister with the diagnosis and themselves, both now and in the future
- All families are different and the needs of individual families will vary
- The members of the wider family can be of great support in terms of balance and objectivity and in the occasional crisis

# 3

# Autism: some key facts

This chapter presents some basic facts about autistic spectrum disorder and its links to other conditions. It also considers issues around the assessment, diagnosis and prevalence of autism and discusses associated health issues.

## Some key facts

Let's start with some very positive characteristics that may be found in children and adults with autism:

- Absolute loyalty and devotion to others close to them
- 'Stickability' at a task will often make them excellent employees in adulthood
- Capacity to view the world in unusual (and often enriching) ways. This attention to detail can be found in areas such as music, mechanical tasks, art, etc.
- Can process visual information better than that given purely in spoken form
- Can concentrate for long periods on a single activity, when it is of interest to them
- Succeed, if they are more able, in academic areas that do not require high degrees of social understanding and where the language used is technical or mathematical (e.g. science, engineering, music, IT). (Based in part on Jones, Jordan and Morgan, 2001.)

'Autism' is a term that has come into prominence during the past 50 years or so. Based upon a Greek word meaning 'withdrawn', it was used first in 1944 by an Austrian psychiatrist, Leo Kanner, to describe a group of people who presented with similar profiles. These characteristics were encapsulated during the 1970s by Lorna Wing and Judy Gould into three key areas, known as 'the triad of impairments', so that today we see that individuals with autism are affected in their ability to:

- understand and use non-verbal and verbal communication
- interpret social behaviour, which in turn affects their ability to interact with other children and with adults
- think and behave flexibly (i.e. to know how to adapt their abilities and areas of strengths and weaknesses).

We also know now that children with autism may have motor co-ordination, perceptual, organisational and sensory difficulties. (There is more information about the impact of sensory differences in Chapter 6.)

## Assessment and diagnosis

The question occasionally asked is whether having a diagnosis with autism is important. The answer must be 'Yes', as a diagnosis may be the gateway to gaining contact with other families; to membership of parent groups; to the most appropriate information and support. Being able to find out more and to understand the reasons for your child's behaviour and the way he perceives the world around him is going to be extremely important in helping to devise strategies to assist him. You must be careful, though, to take into account your child's unique individual personality and the environment in which he lives and learns.

The process of assessing a child for autism and giving a diagnosis can take place as early as 18 months of age. Often the signs may be picked up by health visitors, nursery nurses and other frontline health workers who will listen carefully to parents' concerns. Sometimes screening tools are used which are simply short checklists that may lead to a suggestion that autism may be present and that more in-depth assessments may be needed. Realistically though, this awareness of autism may not always be as proficient in all locations and in all individual cases, and there is still the need for training of professionals to recognise that a child may be displaying signs of autism.

There is widespread international recognition of autistic spectrum disorders, which are classified by two main systems: the International

Classification of Diseases, 10th Revision, (ICD 10) by the World Health Organisation and the *Diagnostic and Statistical Manual* IV (DSM IV) by the American Psychiatric Association. Both systems are currently being updated and both employ the 'triad of impairments' as the core characteristics for the diagnosis of autism.

Occasionally parents may hear the term 'autistic tendencies' being used by clinicians. If so, they must not be 'fobbed off' and insist on clarification, as the term 'autistic tendencies' is not very helpful and reflects indecision on the part of the professionals. Here are some common terms families may hear:

- Kanner's syndrome
- Asperger syndrome (*note*: pronounced with hard 'g'and no 's' at the end)
- high functioning autism
- classical autism

## Association with other conditions

Autistic spectrum disorder can be present in children and adults of any ability and sometimes it can be also found in people with other disabilities such as Down syndrome; phenylketonuria (PKU); Rett syndrome; hypothyroidism; rubella embryopathy; William's syndrome; Tourette syndrome; and tuberous sclerosis. There is also an association of autism with mental health difficulties, and adults with Asperger syndrome are especially vulnerable to depression resulting largely from social isolation.

Epilepsy is fairly common in autism and can manifest in various forms. In studies of autism and epilepsy in the very young, those children with associated moderate or severe learning disabilities had around a fifth to a third chance of developing epilepsy (Wainscott and Corbett, 2000).

## How common is autism?

This is a frequently asked question but, unfortunately, it is difficult to answer accurately. We do know that the prevalence of autism is far higher than many of the other conditions that we hear about so regularly in the media. Indeed, autism is more common than Down syndrome, multiple sclerosis and cerebral palsy combined. In Wales alone, which has a total population of just over 3 million, there are at least 20,000 children and adults with autism. If we add to this figure the same number of families affected by autism and those who work with children with autism in mainstream and specialist schools, in nurseries, as health professionals, etc., we will find that over 2 per cent of the population of Wales is connected either directly or indirectly with autism, i.e. around 55,000 people. With such a large number of people affected by autism it is perhaps not surprising that there are over 200 charities throughout the UK working in the field of autism.

For parents there are clear advantages of such a large community for autism in the UK. At a local level there is likely to be a support group in the area, usually led by parents themselves. There is a big body of literature in book and leaflet format and on the internet, from which you can glean considerable information about autism. A list of some of the most valuable resources in terms of national charities (each UK country has one), internet sources, helplines and publications can be found at the end of this book.

## Is the experience of autism the same for families in other countries?

Internationally, in many countries the experience of families living with autism has been quite similar and the following factors seem to apply:

- no country in the world provides a full range of services to support families
- where services have been available, these have largely resulted from the efforts of interested 'professionals' and especially from the hard work of parents
- progress of service developments has been very slow and it would appear that services for adults begin to develop many years after children's services have been developed – yet, individuals with autism live far longer as adults than as children.

## Health needs of children with autism

The child and adult with autism will have the same health needs as any person within the general population. A particular difficulty with a child or indeed an adult with autism is recognising when he is ill, as the signs may not be suspected initially. The person with autism is unlikely to be able to describe any pain from various parts of the body or, indeed, just when they are feeling generally poorly. Changes from the usual patterns of behaviour may be a critical sign that something is physically wrong and needs checking out by a GP. The need to explore physical reasons as a first course of explanation when the behaviour of the person with autism suddenly changes is a key message that applies not just to parents but also to those who work with children in schools, nurseries, and so on.

Taking your son or daughter to the doctor, dentist or optician can be a trial in itself and not least for the person carrying out the assessment! In recent years many GP surgeries and dentists have become more in tune with autism and far more sensitive to the needs of individuals with autism.

## Preventative health

There are several strands making up good preventative health practice for children and adults with autism and these will include the need, as with every other child, for immunisation, the testing of sight and hearing and good preventative dental health.

### Hearing

Taking hearing first, autism is recognised as a key communication disorder and so accurate assessment of hearing is a vital task to be undertaken early on in the life of the child with autism. Remember also that while the primary role of assessment of a young child's hearing by visiting health visitors to the family home is to ascertain whether the child responds to various sounds, it is important to rule out that the child is sensitive to over-amplification of sound, which may be in itself extremely upsetting to the non-deaf child with autism.

Indeed, it is often the parents themselves who initiate the need for assessments of their child's hearing because of their apparent lack of attention and selective hearing. Sounds or phrases that appear of no value to us can often be most interesting to the child with autism.

Alternatively, a person with autism may sometimes push their fingers in their ears or cup their hands across the outside of the ear and this may be an indication of hypersensitivity to sound or indeed of auditory overload. Soothing music can sometimes be used as a practical strategy in this situation and MP3 players or personal disc players can be helpful in some circumstances in terms of deflecting away from the disruptive noise and replacing with something more conducive to the hearing of the child.

### Dental health

Regular contact with a local dentist before dental problems arise is essential. This will help the dentist to begin to prepare and adapt his approach in terms of assessing the child with autism and, equally, it will help the child to become familiar with both the dentist and the environment of the dental surgery. Individuals with autism may have specific dental needs in circumstances where there may be grinding of the teeth and the placing in the mouth of dirty objects from the environment (known as 'pica'). It is recognised that people with autism may have very particular eating habits and indeed insist upon sameness in diet. The effect over a long period of time of a high-carbohydrate diet may be to predispose to gum disease and not least to general nutritional deficiencies and ill-health. The earlier that the child with autism becomes accustomed to eating a wide and healthy diet the better, as the longer a restricted diet continues, the greater the potential damage to health and continuation of the habit into adulthood. However, some people with autism also have an intolerance to gluten and/or casein (found in dairy products) so this also needs to be taken into account.

### Sight

Many writers with an autistic spectrum disorder report that their sight can be distorted from time to time, causing them concern and worry. If a child with ASD does not wish to go into a room or other setting, it may well be because of a dislike of lighting, humidity or temperature.

One video which parents may find useful is Channel 4's 'A is for Autism', which provides good examples of the types of visual disturbances that people with ASD may experience. (Available at sites such as **www.amazon.co.uk.**)

It is quite usual for people with ASD to have some strong preferences and dislikes in terms of colours, symmetry and sequencing. Behind this perceptual need for 'sameness' may be an inherent desire for security and, as long as this does not interfere abnormally with everyday life, these personal experiences should be respected by all of us. However, when the need for sameness infringes upon their quality of life in a very negative and frequent way, then strategies need to be employed, and suggested approaches are detailed in Chapter 6.

### Exercise

Parents and those who have worked with children and adults with autistic spectrum disorders over many years recognise the value of physical activity – even strenuous activity – in helping to reducing stress and anxiety in children and adults with autism.

## Points to remember

- A diagnosis of an autistic spectrum disorder can be a signpost for the type of services that may be most helpful
- People with ASD can have tremendously positive personal characteristics which can be of benefit to families, schools and, later in life, to employers
- We need to be aware that individuals with ASD can have a hypersensitivity to certain smells, sounds and touch, and to visual disturbances which can have an effect upon their lives. We should respect these individual differences
- ASD may be associated with other conditions, including mental health difficulties and epilepsy
- Autism is a world-wide issue impacting upon families in similar ways throughout the globe
- Preventative health by regular visits to the dentist, optician, etc. is as vitally important for the child with autism as any other child

# Getting your child's educational needs met

This chapter gives some information about the help you can expect in school and from your local authority in getting the educational support your child needs.

All children learn in different ways and may have different levels of special educational need (SEN). The help they need in school will vary accordingly. Every educational setting has to have an SEN policy in place, setting out how that school or nursery will go about meeting a child's needs, and there must also be a Special Educational Needs Co-ordinator (SENCo), who carries the responsibility of ensuring the policy is adhered to on an everyday basis, and an SEN governor for parents to raise concerns with.

In the first instance, it is the role of the class teacher to identify your child's needs, use different methods to meet those needs, and monitor your child's progress, through careful observation and recording. Your own involvement at every stage in this ongoing process is vital, as you are the expert on your child, and his/her needs will be best met by a partnership approach between you and school staff.

If your child does not make progress within a reasonable time, you and school staff together may decide further support is needed. This is called Early Years Action in early years settings and School Action for children over statutory school age. An Individual Education Plan (IEP) will be drawn up, setting achievable targets for your child that have been agreed between you and school staff, and there will be regular reviews to monitor progress. Your child should also have an opportunity to contribute to the reviews.

If your child continues to have difficulties, the school may take advice from external services such as the Learning Support Service, an educational psychologist or speech and language therapist. Involving professionals from outside the school in this way is called Early Years Action Plus or School Action Plus.

Some children may still continue to have significant needs that cannot be met from the school's own resources or by involving other professionals. In such cases, a request for Statutory Assessment of SEN may be made. This calls for a more detailed assessment of your child's needs. Usually, the request is made jointly by the school, parents and professionals working with the child, but parents have the right to make a request themselves. If you think your child needs a Statutory Assessment and want to make such a request, you can do it in one of two ways:

1. Approach the school and ask the head to request assessment. *Beware*! There is no recourse to the Special Educational Needs and Disability Tribunal (SENDIST) if the school has requested the assessment.
2. Contact the local education authority directly and request assessment. The LEA must comply with your request unless your child has been assessed in the last six months or the LEA decides it is not necessary, having looked at all the evidence. If the LEA refuses an assessment, you can appeal to SENDIST.

Having agreed to make an assessment, the LEA gathers evidence about your child's needs from the school, an educational psychologist, the health authority, social services and any other relevant professionals who know your child. Parents are also invited to send in a report, giving their views of their child's needs. The assessment should take no more than 26 weeks to complete. (See the chart at the end of this chapter for a breakdown of the timescales.) Once all the reports have been completed, the LEA decides whether or not to issue a Statement. If no Statement is issued, you can appeal to the Tribunal against that decision.

If the LEA undertakes a formal assessment and decides to issue a Statement, you will receive a Proposed Statement. This should set out all of your child's needs and the provision required to meet those needs. It is essential that you check the Proposed Statement very carefully to ensure that all your child's needs will be met within the LEA's recommended type of provision for your child. If you do not agree with the provision the LEA is recommending because you feel it cannot meet all your child's needs, you can ask for the recommended provision to be changed.

The LEA will not name a school on the Proposed Statement. At this point you have the right to express a preference for the school of your choice, but the LEA does not have to accept your suggestion, especially if your choice is an independent school. You may, however, contest the LEA's choice of placement named on the Final Statement by appealing to SENDIST. The evidence you need to show, that none of the LEA's schools can meet your child's needs, may be found on the reports submitted during assessment by professionals who know your child. If not, you may need to seek an independent professional opinion to back up your case from someone who has met and assessed your child and visited the school(s) in question.

If a Statement of SEN is issued, it will be reviewed at least once a year (annual review), to monitor your child's progress, review and set targets, as appropriate, and check that the educational provision remains suitable to meet your child's ongoing needs. You can request more frequent reviews if you think it necessary.

Every area has a Parent Partnership Service to assist parents through this long and complicated process. You can also get help through various voluntary organisations; see the final chapter of this book for more information.

## Points to remember

 You can appeal to SENDIST if the LEA:

- Refuses to assess a child, or to re-assess when no assessment has been made for six months
- Refuses to issue a Statement after formal assessment or ceases to maintain the Statement
- Describes a child's needs or recommends provision in a Statement that parents disagree with or refuses to provide the level of support parents feel the child needs
- Refuses to name the school that parents feel will meet the child's needs, does not name a school or recommends a school that parents feel is unsuitable

## The process and time limit for making assessments and statements of special educational needs

(Adapted from the Special Educational Needs Code of Practice)

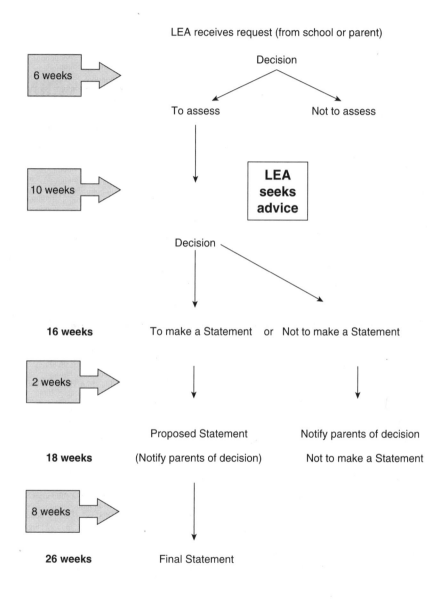

LEA receives request (from school or parent)

Decision

6 weeks

To assess                                    Not to assess

LEA seeks advice

10 weeks

Decision

16 weeks          To make a Statement    or   Not to make a Statement

2 weeks

Proposed Statement              Notify parents of decision

18 weeks          (Notify parents of decision)           Not to make a Statement

8 weeks

26 weeks          Final Statement

# Choosing a school

This chapter considers the factors to be taken into account in choosing a school for a child on the autistic spectrum and suggests questions families may want to ask in making this all-important decision. The chapter closes with some pointers about securing a place at an autism-specific independent special school, if appropriate.

Choosing a school for a child with an autistic spectrum disorder may feel like the biggest decision families have to make. There is a real sense of needing to 'get it right' because your child only gets one chance at education and if you make the 'wrong' choice, s/he may not make progress and fulfil their potential.

The difficulty in choosing a school for any child is that all children are different – never is this truer than for children with ASD – and finding the school setting to suit each child is therefore problematic. Governmental initiatives for raising standards in schools and the push towards inclusion for all makes the choice even harder and, of course, the question of school 'choice' is somewhat of a misnomer, as local educational provision will depend very much on the availability of different types of school in a given area, local authority policy on placement of children with SEN, funding, staffing and resource issues – all of which are often beyond the control of individual families. Parents can 'state a preference' for a particular school but cannot demand a place at their chosen school if the local authority thinks otherwise.

However, sometimes even getting to the point of feeling confident about what you want for your child's education is a big hurdle. Some parents are adamant that they want a mainstream school for their child; others are equally certain that only a special school will fit the bill, while yet others are completely confused about what is on offer and what will meet their child's needs. Let's consider some of the fundamental questions you need to ask yourself about your views on your child's education in the big debate of mainstream versus specialist provision:

- Will my child cope with the academic work of a mainstream school?
- Will my child cope with the social side of a mainstream school – playtime, lunch break, after school clubs?
- What is important to me? Easy access to appropriate role models? One-to-one support? Independent living skills? Social skills? Academic success? Sensory issues?
- Will my child be able to understand the teacher's instructions and expectations?
- How will I know if s/he is happy/is making progress?

**REFLECTIVE OASIS**

Do I believe all children should be educated in their local school and be included, no matter what?

What implications does this have in choosing a school for my child?

Do I believe that my child's needs can be better met in a specialist setting?

What support am I seeking for my child?

Consider the 4-year-olds in the following case studies.

---

**CASE STUDY**

**Ahmed**

Very bright and precocious, he is very interested in dinosaurs and talks about them all the time – his knowledge is extensive and impressive but he doesn't know when to drop the subject. His level of language is way above that of his peer group and he gets on better with adults, who appreciate his sophisticated use of language and his quirky sense of humour. He doesn't suffer fools gladly, has to be right all the time, cannot tolerate factual errors and will happily correct other children – and adults – if he sees they have made a mistake. He finds it hard to make friends and when things don't go his way he can be aggressive. He finds it hard to follow instructions, and teachers find his behaviour intolerable at times. He will not accept authority and is very self-directed.

---

**CASE STUDY**

**Emma**

Placid, calm and well-behaved, she is a very 'biddable' child who does as she is told. She is very quiet and appears to have very little spoken language. Her nursery staff have queried 'elective mutism'. Mum reports that she doesn't say much at home either. She is very shy and seems fearful of her own shadow. She doesn't stand up for herself and allows other children to boss her around. She will not assert what she wants and does not complain if another child snatches a toy away from her – she would not 'say boo to a goose'. She follows the herd, not showing any initiative, and she is often found hiding under tables and in the home corner. A very passive child, she will sit for ages staring into space and doing nothing.

**Tommy**

He is completely non-verbal, and it is difficult to work out how much he understands of what is going on around him. A 'tornado child', always 'on the go', running, climbing, jumping, he pulls toys off shelves and wreaks havoc in his wake. With no sense of danger, he needs constant supervision or he ends up breaking things and/or hurting himself. Very much on his own agenda, he spends hours at the sand tray but cannot sit still at story-time and is always wandering off. He cannot bear being touched and will 'lash out' at other children if they come too close or try to play with him. Loud noises upset him and he will throw himself onto the floor screaming, bite his hand or bang his head into the wall at the slightest provocation. He throws things if an adult tries to involve him in an activity.

Do you think all three children would benefit from the same kind of educational provision? And what about your child? What kind of school will be most appropriate?

## Questions to ask yourself when looking around a school

### Environment

Children with autism get anxious and confused in unfamiliar environments. Consider the following about the school overall:

- Size and layout of the buildings and the campus. Split site? Split levels? Open plan or self-contained classrooms? Specialist areas? Play/recreation areas?
- Space – too much, or too little? Cramped classrooms? Narrow corridors?
- Where do pupils eat?
- Where does one-to-one work take place?
- Noise levels. Are there quiet places your child can go as a 'bolthole' if it all gets too much?

- Sensory issues: lighting, acoustics, 'smell' of certain rooms, e.g. science labs, dining hall.
- Condition of toilet and cloakroom facilities?
- Safety issues: are there clear boundaries (fences, physical barriers) in the playground, to keep children from absconding? A security system to keep out intruders?

### Staffing

It is important that all staff that encounter your child understand the nature of autism and its implications for learning. This includes admin and support staff, the caretaker, lunchtime supervisors and taxi escorts. Consider the following:

- How many staff do you see around the school and what are they doing?
- Do the staff you meet seem knowledgeable about autism?
- What training have they had on autism and how interested do they seem in your child and getting relevant information from you?

### Pupils

The proximity and interaction of other children can 'make or break' the experience of school for your child. Consider:

- General class size, size of sets/groups for specific subjects. Will your child get enough individual attention?
- Seating arrangements: Individual? Groups? Large or small tables? At random? Scope for an independent workstation if that is what your child needs?
- Groupings: Mixed ability? Setting? Streaming? Withdrawal work? One-to-one support?
- Movement around the school: Jostling? Calm and ordered? Dinner queue? Playground behaviour?
- Social activity: What do you observe? Do children work/play co-operatively? What about those who don't want to join in?

### Ethos

It is important that you feel welcome and that your child does too. Consider:

- How are you made to feel?
- How do staff communicate with pupils?
- How do pupils treat each other?
- How do you see children with obvious difficulties being treated?
- What support systems are in place for children who need help?
- What access does the school have to outside help from visiting professionals?
- What is the school's anti-bullying policy?
- How are children punished or reprimanded?
- Is there anything that makes you cringe?
- How are they praised and rewarded?
- Are they given responsibilities around school, to make them feel valued?
- Are the staff aware of the Good Practice Guidelines to what makes an ASD-friendly school?

### Curriculum

You will want to know your child is learning and making progress. Flexibility with regard to the curriculum is vital. Consider:

- National Curriculum: How is it all covered? Set programme of work? Does my child have to do all subjects? How is the work broken down differently (differentiated) for individual pupils?
- Classroom activity: What work is going on? Is it purposeful? Do the pupils seem to know what they are doing? Are all children doing the same or different tasks? Is anybody doing nothing? How are staff supporting the activities?
- Learning styles and teaching methods: Are children expected to follow mainly verbal instructions? Do you see any evidence of visual support? Is there variety of task/activity and flexibility of approach, reflecting the different ways children learn? How will your child ask for help?
- Timetable: Can you see a timetable on display? How do children know what they have to do, how long for and what will happen next? How are supply teachers briefed about the needs of individual children and the timetable to be followed? What happens when there are unexpected disruptions to the timetable?

### Parental involvement

A partnership approach between home and school is essential if children are to get the most out of their educational experience. Consider:

- Information: How will the school keep you informed about what is going on at school and about your child's progress? Open days? Opportunities to view work children have done? Special events? Home/school diaries to monitor everyday events, check information and share minor worries? How easy is it to access relevant staff to ask questions and share concerns?
- Involvement: How does the school involve parents? What activities are arranged for parents to attend? What evidence do you see that parents are welcome in school? Open-door policy? Arrangements for IEP reviews and target-setting? Annual and transition reviews?

## Securing a place at an autism-specific independent special school

If you do not feel that your child's current school meets his/her needs and you want the specialist provision offered by an autism-specific independent (non-maintained) special school, possibly in a residential placement, to find an appropriate school you can try:

- consulting your LEA's list of local special schools
- consulting the Register of Educational Establishments (Tel. 0207 403 0507); a database of all educational establishments in England is maintained on behalf of the DfES.

You have found the right school. What next? How can you secure a place? Your child must have a Statement of Special Educational Needs in order to expect a local education authority to fund an educational placement for your child at any special school. If your child already has a Statement, you need to check it carefully to ensure that it still represents an accurate description of your child's needs and of the appropriate provision required to meet those needs. If it does not, you can request a reassessment, with a view to obtaining a change of placement to reflect your child's changing needs.

You can 'make representation' to your LEA for the school you want. If your LEA agrees with your choice of school, they can make formal enquiries about availability of places. Most independent special schools need to be approached formally. The school will need to look at the Statement to check that the child's needs match the provision they offer. If the child's needs meet the school's admissions criteria, and the school has a vacancy, the admissions procedure can be started once the funding has been agreed. However, the LEA may not agree with your choice of school for one or more of the following reasons:

- it is not considered suitable to meet your child's needs
- funding the placement would not represent 'an efficient use of resources' (i.e. it would cost too much)
- the LEA believes it possible to meet your child's needs from within its own provision.

If you cannot get the LEA's agreement that your child needs the educational placement you want, you may need to appeal to SENDIST.

There is no obligation on a local education authority to provide the **best** education for your child, only an adequate education to meet the child's needs, as set out in the Statement. If you want your child to attend a specialist independent special school, you have to prove that the LEA's choice of school cannot meet your child's needs **at all**, not that the school of your choice will provide a better education than the school the LEA recommends.

To do this, you will need to gather as much evidence as possible from the professionals who know your child, in order to prove that your child needs specialist input at an independent special school, especially if you are seeking a residential placement. People who may be helpful in providing reports include:

- paediatrician
- psychiatrist
- speech therapist
- clinical psychologist
- educational psychologist
- medical officer for the Local Health Authority Children's Disability Team (or equivalent) from social services.

To be successful at appeal, you will have to show that your child's special educational needs include the need for the range of activities, structures and approaches used within the school of your choice. Having spelt out your child's needs and the provision required to meet those needs, you will need to present evidence that the LEA's choice of school cannot make the provision necessary to meet your child's needs, as you have described them. To prove this, you may need a second professional opinion on the provision available in the LEA school.

The basic principles underlying the law on special education are that individual children's needs are identified, assessed, described in a Statement and then provided for. If your child's needs are fully described in Part 2 of the Statement and the exact provision to meet those needs is specified in detail in Part 3, you should have a good basis for demonstrating that the LEA's choice of school cannot make that provision.

For further information and support, see the final chapter of this book.

## Points to remember

- All children with ASD are different, so an educational setting that suits one child may not suit another
- Children's needs change, so the level of support s/he needs now may be different at a later stage
- The prognosis later in life is better for those children who receive appropriate support and intervention earlier on
- If your observations and the answers you get to questions when visiting a school make you feel uneasy, trust your intuition – this may not be the best place for your child
- If the school seems reluctant to accept your child, ask yourself: do I really wish my child to attend a school that doesn't want him?
- You will get a 'feel' for the school that might accommodate your child's needs best – a welcoming atmosphere, a willingness to be flexible, a sense of being listened to and that they want to get to know you and your child and work with you for your child's best interests

# Positive strategies for daily living

This chapter considers the reasons underlying the behaviour of children with autism at home and out in the community and suggests some strategies for managing difficulties and developing positive communication and interaction.

Living with a child with autism can be daunting and stressful, although ultimately very rewarding. You may find some behaviour perplexing and challenging, and ways you have found to manage the behaviour of other children in the family may not work with your child with autism. What can you do to stop the family home becoming a battleground and begin to enjoy life with your child more?

First of all, understanding why behaviour is happening is important. Children with autism are children first, so their behaviour may well have the same reasons as with any other child, e.g. wanting something they can't have, not wanting to go to bed, but, unlike other children, they are less likely to do something just to get your attention. More likely, if it seems like that, they are trying to impose their own control on a world they find bewildering by behaving in ways which will get a predictable response from you that they find reassuring. This helps them make sense of their confusion and anxiety in a world they don't understand.

## Coping with change and the need for predictability

At home it is very difficult, if not impossible, to keep things the same and avoid change. However, this is no bad thing, because our children need to learn how to cope with the unexpected and how to move successfully from one setting to another. If we try to keep things the same and never challenge the child's need for sameness, he will never learn to be flexible – an essential life skill. We need to find a balance between enough predictability, stability and continuity to make a child with autism feel secure, but not so much that it adds to the already rigid thinking and behaviour that characterise autism.

A prime reason for behaviour difficulties in a child with autism is anxiety, often caused by the child not knowing what he should be doing or what is going to happen next, by unfamiliarity of people, places and activities and the expectations of others. Anxiety may spill over into anger, frustration and what looks like aggression but is really a reaction to feeling overwhelmed. Compulsive questioning and commenting may be very irritating but are better tolerated if we know they are caused by anxiety.

A calm, uncluttered environment is most conducive to the well-being of someone on the autism spectrum, but that doesn't describe the average family home. Similarly, having the whole day planned out at the weekend may feel too regimented, but we need to acknowledge the need for some degree of structure and look for ways to achieve a higher level of clarity, consistency, predictability and planned changes to routine, without sacrificing the spontaneity of family life – a tall order! TEACCH (**www.teacch.com**) is an approach that can be adapted in the home to provide some structure.

## Repetitive, stereotyped and obsessive activities

An insistence on elaborate and inflexible routines and rituals is usually the child's way of coping with change and transitions. Letting him hold on to a favoured 'security' toy, especially when doing something new, may help minimise anxiety. Some people try to eliminate obsessions, but the danger is that it may be replaced by something worse. In any case, he may need some time to 'be autistic' as a coping strategy in a world he finds stressful, and the function of behaviour we see as repetitive and purposeless might be an attempt to keep calm, so he will get even more distressed if the coping strategy is not allowed.

It is usually better to look for ways to 'box the obsession', i.e. by setting clear boundaries around when, where and for how long the activity is allowed – maybe using it as a reward for having done another activity that the child isn't so keen on (washing up? homework?). Children with ASD find unusual things rewarding, e.g. a piece of string to twiddle, the opportunity to examine the drains, and being allowed some 'chill-out' time to indulge in 'stimming' behaviours and stereotyped activities can be very relaxing for them. It is too demanding to expect them to do meaningful activities all the time, so aim for a balance of purposeful activity (adult-led) and relaxing activities (child-led) and allow time to indulge in harmless obsessions and ritualistic behaviours.

## Sensory issues

Children with autism may have problems with balance, spatial awareness and a sense of their own self. These difficulties, combined with no sense of danger, may cause difficulties at home and out and about. They are often sensory avoiders or sensory seekers and this may fluctuate from day to day, causing many different difficulties:

- The inability to filter out irrelevant sensory stimuli may lead to screaming or withdrawal – sensory overload from too much noise, from smells, lights, crowds, etc.
- Fascination with sensory stimuli  may lead to inappropriate grabbing and touching.
- Exploratory play may lead to destruction of possessions, smearing.
- The feel of certain fabrics may cause the child to strip clothing, rip out labels or take off shoes all the time.
- Faddy eating because of taste and texture of foods; visual appearance of food on plate.
- Personal hygiene issues – not liking to be touched or cuddled; encroachment of personal space; invasive nature of activities like brushing teeth, cutting toe nails, washing hair, smell of the toilet. Parents need to be aware of these sensitivities but also realise that because you cannot make a child eat, sleep or use the toilet on demand, it is best to remain calm, positive and seemingly nonchalant. If the child thinks that you think it's a big deal, he will make the most of the control it gives him.
- Self-injury – head banging, biting his own hand, etc. These activities are distressing to watch but give the child sensory feedback twice over and induce a feeling of calm. Parents need to find another way of providing similar sensations without the harm. Exercise and rhythmic movement are good for this – try jogging or brisk walking, trampolining, swings, gentle rocking, rolling him up tightly in a blanket or duvet.

**REFLECTIVE OASIS**

Many different reasons may cause the same behaviour. Consider some possible reasons for a child having a tantrum:

- wanting something he can't have
- reaction to something he dislikes
- avoidance tactic
- anger
- fear
- frustration
- distress
- over-sensitivity to sensory stimuli – noise disturbance (echoing church hall, crowded shop, vacuum cleaner, traffic)
- change of place, routine; unfamiliar person or event; lack of understanding of what's happening.

Before you can decide what to do about the behaviour, you have to work out the most likely reason for it happening. How can you work it out? What would you do for each of the above possibilities?

## Communication and social interaction

These are closely linked – a two-way process between at least two people. For effective communication you need three things:

- Why? – the motivation to communicate
- What? – something to communicate about
- How? – means (speech, signing, pictures/symbols, the written word).

The 'why' and the 'what' are the most important at first. It is no good having any communication system if you do not have something to communicate or the desire to do so. This is the crux of the matter with autism – not feeling the desire to communicate or interact with others, not attending to others or finding them interesting, means that autistic children often do not realise they can have an influence or effect on others by what they say and do and they therefore may not intentionally direct their communicative behaviour towards others. Of course, they may still communicate unintentionally through their behaviour, but this is 'hit and miss', depending on the other person knowing them well and being able to 'read' their behaviour. Quite often, even when they do have something to communicate, they do not realise they have to get someone's attention first, or they lack the language skills to let you know they are uncomfortable, unwell, afraid, wet, clothes are too tight or the sun is in their eyes...

Some children speak very well, others poorly or not at all. Processing speech is stressful and exhausting for even the most able person on the autism spectrum. We know their level of understanding is likely to lag behind their own use of speech, making people think they understand more than they do, and it's not only the spoken language that is a problem, but also non-verbal communication. This includes facial expression, tone of voice, body movement, gesture, intonation patterns, posture and eye contact. Babies use this effectively in the first two years of life, but it is still important after speech is learnt – giving us the emotional messages of how people are feeling or reacting to us. All people with ASD have trouble with non-verbal communication, especially if they have a learning difficulty as well, so they may only communicate basic needs and wants, not how they are feeling, and will struggle to understand this from others.

Spoken language is transient, whereas pictures and symbols are permanent and visual, which helps people with ASD make sense of things. This is why the Picture Exchange Communication System (PECS) can be so useful (**www. pecs.com**). The usual stages of communication for someone on the autism spectrum will be to relate to 3D objects first, then move on to photos, pictures and symbols, to written words and eventually to the spoken word.

**REFLECTIVE OASIS**

How can we make sure we are communicating with our children at the level they understand?

How can we help effective communication happen?

***Communication tips***

- Be sensitive to attempts to communicate and set up situations to encourage it. Try not to anticipate or pre-empt needs/wants, so that the child has to try. For example, keep toys on a high shelf he can't reach or behind (locked) glass door, so he has to 'ask' through eye pointing, finger pointing, reaching for item, vocalising, signing or naming, according to his communication level.
- Use speech economically: simplify language; use short sentences; give one instruction at a time, not a sequence; use intonation sparingly; leave pauses and give time to respond.
- Make your meaning clear: say what you mean and mean what you say; name first to get attention; say sentences in the right order; use concrete, not abstract, concepts; avoid inferred, implied meaning; avoid 'no' and 'don't'; avoid or explain idioms that may be taken literally; use visual supports to aid understanding and keep body language to a minimum.
- Use a firm, direct approach: child may not respond if the adult is hesitant; show what you mean, rather than telling; avoid opportunity to refuse, e.g. 'Come and ride this bike', not 'Do you want to ride this bike?'; limit choice of visual items and remove choice altogether for 'invisible' choices, e.g. 'We're going to the park' not 'Do you want to go to the park or the shops?'

## Developing play and social skills

Children with ASD play differently from other children. They may have odd patterns of looking at things or spend a long time scrutinising a toy or part of a toy. They may mouth or sniff toys and spend a lot more time on simple manipulative play rather than symbolic or functional play, even taking into account that they are developmentally young. Their play may be repetitive and stereotyped – lining things up, wanting the same book, game or video over and over again, lacking in novelty and variety and showing unusual responses to some objects – either fascinated or frightened.

Reasons for all this may be linked to sensory issues: having their own sense of order and logic; having too much of an eye for detail at the expense of the 'big picture'; finding the world so confusing that even changing a toy or game seems too risky or scary; not understanding the function of toys or looking to an adult to demonstrate how to use an object; having poor communication, imaginative and imitation skills.

In addition, children with ASD often lack understanding of the necessary concepts to develop appropriate interaction:

- time
- 'finished'
- 'what's next?'
- social timing
- personal space
- appropriate body contact
- friendship
- choices
- how to give and ask for help
- waiting
- sharing
- turn-taking
- recognising and expressing own likes and dislikes – when they want an activity to start, continue or stop
- 'meet and greet'
- initiating activities and recognising invitations to join in
- adapting own behaviour to social situations and following social rules
- organising and sequencing thoughts and actions
- remembering and using coping strategies
- problem-solving.

## How can we help?

There is a difference between the child who is happy to play alone and the child who wants to join in and doesn't know how to. Adults need to find ways of teaching the child with ASD that interacting with others can be fun, by encouraging shared interest, joint attention and participation but not forcing the issue. Warning in advance of an activity stopping or changing and having clear rules for interaction will help the child feel less anxious.

Children with ASD need to be taught how to play rather than being taught through play, and parents need to go back to basics with lots of manipulative and exploratory play before trying to move on to functional – symbolic – social play. It is important to start where the child is and what motivates him, rather than what you think he should be playing with at that age. Regular playtimes at his level will become part of his routine and time spent together, and eye contact, closeness and co-operation can increase gradually.

Useful starting points are tactile play with sand, water, dough; 'cause and effect' toys with novelty elements like flashing lights and sound effects;

musical instruments and toys; lap rhymes (start with back towards you, then at edge of knees, then face to face); also floor games, rough-and-tumble, chasing, tickling, piggyback games – but try to avoid over-excitement.

To develop sharing and turn-taking, try activities that need two people for maximum fun, e.g. seesaw; swings; throwing/catching ball; pushing car to and fro; 'blowing' games with feathers, bubbles, straws; 'Row Your Boat' and 'Seesaw Margery Daw'; pushing another child in a cart; household tasks; helping you carry things; sharing out sweets 'one for me, one for you', etc.

To get your child interested in playing and interacting with you, try the following:

- Play alongside him (with your own set of toys) and do things you know he'll find interesting, but don't get upset if he gets up and walks away or ignores you completely. Children with autism have good peripheral vision and may be taking in more of this 'parallel play' than you think.
- Imitate what he's doing and watch his reaction.
- Comment on his play so he knows you're interested and that his choices are OK by you, but don't ask questions about what he's doing or try to direct his play. It's more important that he learns to enjoy play and inter-action with you than that he plays 'properly' with the toys.
- Build anticipation into 'Ring a Roses' and stamping games.
- React 'as if' he's showing you something even if he's only carrying it around, and he may start to bring things to show you intentionally.
- Exchange a toy with him.
- Try sharing one toy – his turn will have to be much longer than yours at first. He may feel more secure having you join his activity than trying something new or having you change things.
- Teach function of toy by playing with it yourself.
- Teach 'let's pretend' but be prepared for your child thinking you've gone mad when you drink imaginary tea from an imaginary cup!

---

**REFLECTIVE OASIS**

Consider what your child really likes to spend time doing. Lego? Trains? Colouring in? Running up and down the stairs? How can you get involved with this activity?

How can you build on what he is already doing and extend and develop it?

## Approaches and interventions

There is a vast array of different approaches and interventions available that claim to improve different skills in children with autism and may even promise a 'cure'. Parents are justifiably interested in anything that might help their child's development and may be prepared to invest much time, energy and money in specific strategies. But you need to be careful and find out as much as possible about what the intervention entails and ask other parents whether they have found it beneficial before making your decision. Positive approaches like 'Intensive Interaction' build on connecting with people with autism at their own level and accepting them as they are, rather than trying to change them. 'Son-Rise' (**www.Son-Rise.org**) likewise starts from the principle of 'to love is to be happy with', while some intensive approaches, like Lovaas/ABA (**www.Lovaas.com**), set out to change the child's behaviour. Lack of space prevents any further discussion here but more information about different approaches and interventions can be found on the National Autistic Society (NAS) website (see Chapter 10) and in the book *Approaches to Autism* (NAS, 2001).

The following very useful books may help.

*Teaching Young Children with ASD to Learn – A Practical Guide for Parents and Staff in Schools and Nurseries* (Hannah, 2001)
*How Do You Feel Thomas?* is a new book from NAS (2006), using a common interest in Thomas the Tank Engine to explore emotions for children with ASD.
*Challenging Behaviour and Autism – Making Sense, Making Progress* (Whitaker, 2001)
*A Practical Guide to Intensive Interaction* (Nind and Hewett, 2001)

### Points to remember

- To make sense of behaviour, we need to make sense of autism
- Communication is a two-way process
- The ability to talk does not indicate the same ability to understand
- Play leads to learning but the most important thing is to enjoy your child and have fun
- Exercise caution in choosing an approach or intervention to help your child's development

# Growing up and facing the future

This chapter considers some of the difficulties that occur as young people on the autism spectrum start to grow up and make the move from children's to adult services. It also addresses some of the problems faced by families at this time.

Change always brings fear, anxiety, doubt and uncertainty and coping with change across the life span may feel like walking on shifting sands. At every stage in family life for the family living with autism there are major changes to cope with for everybody. Never is this more true than in the teenage years. Adolescence plus autism makes a difficult time even more difficult and there are important issues to be confronted, such as understanding physical and emotional changes, the need for more independence, for making choices, for learning to deal with sexuality and interpersonal relationships and the importance of developing self-confidence and self-esteem.

## Physical changes

Adolescents with ASD may lack understanding of body changes, physical growth and strength, the need for more food and sleep and lack communication skills to express concerns and fears over the changes they don't understand. The lack of social awareness may make them look different from their peers and they may experience difficulties understanding, expressing and coping with emotions brought about by hormonal changes, sexual tension, mood swings and secret worries.

They may lack judgement in unknown areas of self-care, e.g. shaving, menstruation not know how to ask for help and find it hard to modulate sensory issues, e.g. growing pains, body odour. Sensory issues may cause difficulties in personal self-care, e.g. they need to shower more often but don't want to; to shave and shower all at once may be too much to cope with.

### Strategies that may help

- Use pictures, photos and adults to show body changes in others and themselves
- Re-examine sleep needs, look at eating routines and use exercise
- Use body outline to identify body parts that hurt or are uncomfortable
- Help them recognise changing self in mirror reflection
- Use structure to compensate for judgement difficulties and visual check-lists for self-care
- Introduce reward and incentive systems as motivation for improvements in self-care
- Avoid sensory intrusion by dividing tasks like showering and shaving into different parts of day; plan for menstrual care in small steps
- Provide tension-release activities and teach relaxation techniques
- Have 'routines' and cue cards for expressing negative emotions and strategies for dealing with them while staying in control
- Look for 'warning behaviours' and encourage them to take 'time out' until calm
- Avoid power struggles – try to redirect, distract or ignore; walk away from conflict and try another strategy later.

## Making choices

You need to find a balance between allowing a teenager to have his own way and exerting some control as the adult in the situation. Sometimes choice may not be appropriate, e.g. whether to get up or not on a school day, whether to wash. Make it clear that the choice is about the limit to set on a rule, not the rule itself – e.g. the choice of who to walk with, but he has to walk either way because he needs some exercise; the choice of when to leave an activity, not whether to leave or not.

Most adolescents with ASD find limited choice easier than unlimited. Teach decision-making directly. Start with easy things like food and clothes and use pictures to aid choice. Start with two pictures, with one preferred item and one disliked, then move on to a choice between two preferred items and make it clear that it is either...or – and not both. When choosing between two items has been established, use three pictures. Use cue cards to indicate 'no'.

Use a timer to indicate the duration of an activity. Limit special interests according to context, location, amount of time and who is around, but do allow some time somewhere for the young person to do what s/he wants to do and don't insist on socially appropriate behaviour all the time – nobody does that!

Person-centred approaches should reflect what is important **to** each person and what is important **for** each person. This will reflect the choices to be made.

Don't make too big an issue about age appropriateness. It is better to think in terms of what is appropriate to the social context and allow compromises, e.g. play with dinosaurs at home but not in the restaurant for Sunday lunch when you are 15 years old.

Keep introducing new activities, broadening horizons, but do it slowly, in small steps and one-to-one for each new activity. In social groups, have regular routine activities each time, to provide security, so that new activities that are introduced can be coped with better. Provide visual cues to help with learning the rules of the activity. It is important to have experience of an activity before being presented with choices. How can you choose if you don't know what the choice is?

**REFLECTIVE OASIS**

Think about how much and what kind of choices you offer – make sure they are genuine choices. Does it matter to you which choice he makes? Choosing whether to have marmalade or peanut butter on your toast is not as life changing as whether to go to college or get a job!

## Some other difficulties in developing independence

For a teenager with ASD:

- Community activities are more open-ended and they have a poor concept of time
- They lack the ability to deal with the unexpected, to generalise skills
- They lack social communication and interaction skills to express their own wants and needs and understand those of other people
- Problems with 'black and white' thinking lead to rigidity of thought and behaviour and an intolerance of people breaking the rules
- They lack the ability to see multiple perspectives or to think in flexible, abstract and complex ways. They have difficulties in thinking things through and making connections
- They have problems with generalisation, seeing 'cause and effect' and the impact on other people of what they say and do
- They are increasingly interested in other people and want friends but do not know how to go about it appropriately and have difficulty initiating and sustaining social interaction
- They want to feel they belong but have difficulty following unspoken social rules
- They have difficulty seeing themselves as others see them, so may appear socially inept, e.g. they may have special interests that are not 'cool' to talk about
- They may be very vulnerable in social situations because they have difficulty extracting meaning from what is going on around them and cannot easily judge innuendo, teasing, flirting, jokes or sarcasm
- They want to enjoy new experiences, new people and places but lack age-appropriate skills to exercise judgement wisely – which makes them vulnerable out in the community.

## So what will help?

- Give written guidelines for social behaviour, e.g. what to do when you go to the cinema with a friend (and what not to do). Use discussion for ideas about how and who to date, safe places to meet people, etc. For more able people, also have non-intrusive signals for 'saving face' to avoid the anxiety and embarrassment of not behaving appropriately and being pointed out as behaving inappropriately.
- Use colour change clocks to help with understanding of time.

- Use social stories (**www.thegraycenter.org**) or lists of rules for what to do and not do, to help them understand social situations and the perspective of other people, different consequences from different courses of action.
- Use visual cues to help with social activities and take photographs that can be talked about at home to review events and to make choices of preferred friends for specific activities.
- Teach appropriate ways of asking to join in, suggesting an activity or starting a conversation, appropriate topics to talk about and how to take turns.
- Use a peer advocate.

## Sexuality and interpersonal relationships

It is sometimes embarrassing for families to have to broach issues around sexuality, and it is even more fraught when the young person does not really understand what is going on. In addition, there is a clash between society's attitudes and the behaviour of the person with ASD – behaviour may be seen as deviant and sexual when it's really just a sensory issue.

People with autism are more likely to find sexual gratification in a range of ways that would seem unusual to most people, e.g. fetishes, both because of the sensory element and because they are not so people-oriented and may find objects more satisfactory than a human relationship.

We need to teach what is socially appropriate long before the child becomes an adolescent, or the behaviour will be entrenched. The difference between 'private' and 'public' places is most important and you can begin to teach this from an early age.

As an adolescent, s/he will need private space and time for personal hygiene and sexual exploration but will also need direct teaching of when and where is appropriate for certain activities. Use visual cues and physical structure to make it clear.

Use clear, simple language at a level the person can understand to talk about sexual issues and use pictures to back up what you are saying. Teach which words are regarded as vulgar and not to be used.

Use exercise for tension release before going into situations where the drive to sexual activity would be a problem, e.g. classroom, family living room.

Appropriate touching: make it clear what is appropriate. Make important rules visual so there is no confusion. It may be just a habitual sensory activity – try distraction, having something else to hold.

Use pictures of body parts to emphasise the difference between public and private. It is really difficult to teach who is a stranger and who isn't so make a rule that it's never OK for other people, friends or strangers, to touch private parts unless by invitation.

Be aware that people with autism who like computers may see a lot of 'atypical' sexual behaviour on the internet, which they may see as 'normal' because their experience of social norms is limited. Parents need to monitor internet activity with the person with autism just as with any other child.

Two very useful books are *Talking Together About Growing Up* (Scott and Kerr-Edwards, 2004) and *Talking Together About Sex and Relationships* (Scott and Kerr-Edwards, 2003). Other useful resources include: *Personal Hygiene: What's That Got to Do With Me?* (Crissey, 2005) and *Taking Care of Myself – A Healthy Hygiene, Puberty and Personal Curriculum for Young People with Autism* (Wrobel, 2003). More information about these issues for young people with learning disabilities can be found at: **www.growingand learning.co.uk.**

## The importance of self-awareness for people with autistic spectrum disorders

The nature of ASD may cause mental health issues which impair quality of life, social relationships and sense of well-being and interfere with the ability to learn skills and function appropriately within the community.

Lack of understanding of the world the child lives in and its social rules lead to:

- social exclusion
- marginalisation
- feelings of being overwhelmed by society's demands.

Feeling 'the odd one out' and wanting to be the same as everyone else, but not knowing how to, lead to:

- vulnerability
- isolation
- low self-esteem.

Social and communication difficulties cause:

- frustration
- anxiety
- distress.

Acute sensory sensitivity and compulsive, obsessive behaviour single a person out as different and may cause:

- restrictions to learning of new skills
- limits on accessing opportunities in the community
- feelings of inferiority and inability to conform.

Difficulties with communication, social interaction, imagination and sensory differences may lead to:

- inappropriate behaviour
- passivity and withdrawal from social situations
- anger and violence against self, other people and/or property.

Without self-awareness there may be:

- no acceptance of own strengths and weaknesses
- no sense of value
- lack of confidence
- feeling of uselessness
- feeling 'alien' and excluded
- negative attitude to being 'different'
- low self-esteem and self-worth
- lack of well-being
- pessimism and despair that things are the way they are and cannot alter for the better
- depression.

With awareness comes:

- acknowledgement and acceptance of own difficulties
- sense of value and pride in own strengths and abilities
- confidence
- social status
- social inclusion
- positive attitude to being 'different'
- high self-esteem and self-worth
- positive sense of well-being.
- optimism, sense of purpose and feeling that change can happen
- positive frame of mind.

### When to tell

- When the individual with ASD asks questions
- When he is beginning to show anxiety, distress at feeling 'different', or any of the other negative emotions/behaviours above – or before, if possible
- When other people start to make comments or treat him differently and/or negatively – or before, if possible

### How to tell

- By using personal accounts by other people with ASD as a positive role model, e.g. *Freaks, Geeks and Asperger Syndrome* by Luke Jackson (2003), *Martian in the Playground* by Claire Sainsbury (2000).
- By reading stories like *Blue Bottle Mystery* (Hoopman, 2000), *The Curious Incident of the Dog in the Night Time* (Haddon, 2003), *Of Mice and Aliens* (Hoopman, 2004).
- By one-to-one work on the nature of ASD and what makes an individual special and unique from everyone else, e.g. *I Am Special* by Peter Vermeulen (2000); NAS (1999) booklet *What is Asperger Syndrome and How Will It Affect Me?; Coping: A Survival Guide for People with Asperger Syndrome* by Marc Segar (1997).
- By providing opportunities for the person to ask questions and to talk about anxieties and worries with trusted peers, siblings and adults.
- By demonstrating understanding and tolerance of the difficulties and a genuine desire to help him accept the uniqueness that ASD brings.

---

**REFLECTIVE OASIS**

Self-awareness and building of self-esteem are important for all, with or without ASD and across the whole range of intellectual ability.

How can we help a young person with autism feel valued by the rest of us?

How can you help your son/daughter to develop self-confidence, self-worth and self-esteem?

## Family conflicts

As young people with autism begin to grow up, there are contradictions and conflicts to be faced by their family. Parents want what is best for the child but are often unsure what that is and sometimes what is best for the child is painful for the family – 'letting go' is difficult. Families need to let go but they still want to be part of the young person's life. They want to retain responsibility but need support. They may feel a failure for not coping and have to face their own vulnerability – they are getting older, less strong and less able to cope.

As a result, a residential placement brings relief but also guilt, sadness and pain. Parents gain freedom but lose their child and have to adjust to the loss of feeling needed and valued. They want to protect but need to guard against stifling. They make the moves towards independence but fear for the future. There is also adjustment to the role of 'carer' uncertainty about the balance of how often to visit, have the person with autism home, etc, and support systems may disappear because they revolve around the person with autism, not the family. Families are happy when they find appropriate services but always worrying that they will be cut, reduced, removed – worries about continuity.

Mistrust and worry abound – will professionals have the same understanding as the family? Will they look after the child as well as the family? Will they love him? They need to feel pleased about progress the child makes but it is sometimes difficult to feel pleased if the family isn't around and involved in making progress happen.

All the positives of the placement have to be balanced against a feeling of being 'sidelined' – no longer being the most important people in the child's life, having to share that role with professionals. The loss of the caring role may lead to isolation, 'empty nest syndrome'. Parents may find this leads to a reassessment of their own lives and changes in relationships.

**REFLECTIVE OASIS**

If your son moves to a residential placement or gets a home of his own, how will you participate in his life?

What changes will you introduce in your own life to get used to not having the everyday care of your child, especially if that 'child' is now an adult?

## Points to remember

- Adolescents with autism need help to understand how puberty affects their bodies
- There are important issues to consider about making choices and becoming more independent
- Young people on the autism spectrum need careful teaching about issues relating to sexuality and relationships
- Self-awareness is important for all – and that includes people with ASD
- There are no easy answers – all decisions will lead to some family conflicts

# Working together effectively – families and professionals

This chapter aims to help families and practitioners to gain a better understanding of each other's perspective. It considers what families want from professionals, what professionals want from families, the barriers to a partnership approach and the 'building blocks' of effective partnership.

## What families want from practitioners

- Early diagnosis, intervention and assessment – they want to know what they are dealing with and follow-up support.
- Information – to feel empowered. They need good communication so they don't feel overwhelmed.
- To be listened to, taken seriously and to have their opinion valued – acknowledgement that parents know their own child best and what the needs are.
- A range of services to meet the needs of the child.
- A holistic approach to the needs of the whole family.
- Equal partnership with practitioners for the benefit of the child.
- Recognition of the journey they are on, the battles they have fought and why they have become 'warrior parents' – loud, rude and demanding.
- Tolerance and understanding.
- Time to tell their story.
- Acknowledgement of the stress and worries associated with having a child with a disability in the family.

- Acceptance for the child and the family.
- Well-planned, organised, resourced and co-ordinated services, with a 'keyworker' for continuity of service, to avoid the 'falling off a cliff' feeling.
- Understanding of their needs.
- Equality of opportunity.

## What practitioners want from families

- Civility
- Respect
- Appreciation of their knowledge
- Acknowlegement of their commitment to the child and the family
- Understanding of the constraints they are working under – systems, funding arrangements, inadequate staffing, lack of time.

---

### REFLECTIVE OASIS (FOR PRACTITIONERS)

What do you offer families you work with?

Are you ready to listen to their problems?

Do you make time to explain things?

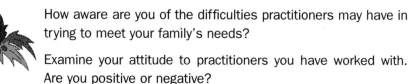

How do you indicate that you value their knowledge and experience?

How do you give them a feeling of participation in their child's life?

What examples of good practice can you think of from your own work setting?

---

### REFLECTIVE OASIS (FOR FAMILIES)

How aware are you of the difficulties practitioners may have in trying to meet your family's needs?

Examine your attitude to practitioners you have worked with. Are you positive or negative?

What do you know of their knowledge and experience?

## Barriers to co-operation

These barriers may exist on one or both sides of the partnership and should be acknowledged so that they can be 'chipped away':

- Superior or patronising attitude
- Lack of respect for the other's point of view
- Lack of understanding of where the other person is coming from
- Prejudice – related to age, gender, race, culture, lifestyle, class, education, job, standing within the community
- Language – genuine difficulties when there is no common language spoken and a need for interpreters, but also metaphorically 'not speaking the same language'
- No shared aims – wanting different things.

## The 'building blocks' of effective partnership

These principles are simple but can make all the difference:

- Mutual respect and tolerance
- A belief in the expertise, knowledge and experience of the other, leading to mutual understanding of where these overlap and complement each other
- A willingness and commitment to working together for the good of the child
- An honest and realistic approach
- Positive communication
- Co-operation towards shared goals
- Flexibility
- Listening skills
- Encouraging strengths rather than always focusing on weaknesses
- Accepting differences.

Families of children with autism are all different and will have reached a different level of awareness of their child's needs and their own. Practitioners need to be aware of that and also of the fact that at least some of the families will be difficult to engage with because they share some of the characteristics of their child – autism has genetic links, after all.

Some parents are cynical, belligerent or seem to be in denial and it is important that practitioners recognise the reasons behind this – the battles for services, the disappointment of promises being broken, the rhetoric but no action that sometimes characterises the services families are trying to access. Understanding these issues will make the practitioner much more tolerant of 'difficult' parents.

Likewise, all practitioners are different and bring their own perspective to the table, positive or negative. Some teachers never intended to work with children with special needs and the governmental push towards inclusion has forced them into a situation they didn't envisage, working with children whose needs they don't necessarily understand and without special training. They may lack confidence but not wish to 'lose face' by acknowledging this to family members.

Other practitioners go out of their way to be helpful and considerate. They go beyond their job remit to make families feel comfortable with protocols and paperwork, to explain jargon and procedures, to inform and empower parents through the ongoing and often bureaucratic educational process.

When there is a real sense of 'being in this together', the most successful partnerships are forged in the best interests of the child/adult with autism at the centre of all the discussion. Let's not lose sight of the mental grind-down, over years, for the family of living with autism and the battles it brings with it. Practitioners who can stick with it for some of the ride with good humour and in the true spirit of partnership will be appreciated. Here's just one typical story, much abbreviated, to give you a flavour of what's at stake.

### CASE STUDY

Simon was a very placid, good-tempered baby. His parents had no concerns until he had a development check at 18 months, when the doctor felt he might be deaf and referred him to a hearing specialist. This was the start of 2½ years of referrals, clinic and hospital appointments and various therapists visiting the family at home and sharing their thoughts and strategies around Simon's needs. By the time he was 4 years old the family were desperate for an answer to the question 'what is wrong with our child?' and were relieved to get a diagnosis of classic autism and a severe learning disability. It had been a long, hard road to get the assessment and diagnosis right and a Statement of Special Educational Needs in place.

*(Continued)*

*(Continued)*

Simon attended a pre-school assessment unit for children with special needs for five terms before starting at the local SLD school. His parents were pleased that his significant needs in self-help, communication and socialisation would be met and were happy for a few years with the progress he made at school in a small class, with a teacher who understood autism. Because he met eligibility criteria for help from social services, a visiting toy library, play-schemes, babysitting service and respite care were also available to the family and a local parent support group, regional and national autism organisations provided the family with useful support.

At age 11 there were difficulties with Simon moving into the secondary unit of the school because he was the only autistic child in the group and his needs were too diverse, his learning profile too patchy. After three nightmare years, an escalation in behaviour that challenged his family and his school staff greatly because he simply couldn't cope, the long battle for re-assessment and a close shave with the SEN Tribunal, he ended up at a specialist residential school. The emotional wrench for his family was tremendous but his five happy years there returned him to the calm, contented lad he'd been before.

At 19 he had to leave that environment and make the move to an adult residential placement far from home because nothing suitable could be found closer to his family. Again the financial battle to get the place he needed, again the emotional turmoil. He's 20 now. Who knows what the next battle will be…

## Points to remember

- True partnership is hard work but very rewarding
- There are two sides to every story and partnership is a two-way street
- 'United we stand, divided we fall' – together families and practitioners can make much more positive difference to the lives of people with autism than they can separately

# Keeping it all in perspective

This chapter considers the impact of autism on the mental and physical health of affected families and makes the case for families needing to find ways to keep sane and get the support they need. It also analyses the role of the media and other factors that have an influence in the lives of these families.

## Mental and physical health issues

- Negative feelings of helplessness, despair; being overwhelmed by circumstances beyond their own control – often compounded by inadequate external support and information.
- Behaviour, communication and social difficulties put additional stress on carers, especially since these problems often get worse, both in prevalence and severity, as children get older and bigger. Lack of confidence in their own ability to cope and fear of the unknown, unexpected and unpredictable add to stress.
- Mental 'grind-down' and stress of fighting for appropriate support and services for the whole family and to obtain provision that meets the child's needs, advice on early intervention and an accurate diagnosis of the child's difficulties – made worse by constant rounds of visits by various professionals and to hospitals and clinics, repeating the same information, alongside the need to provide continual care and supervision for a child with autism.

- Lack of sleep and relaxation because of the child's needs and inadequate provision of respite care that would enable the carer to take a break from the 'juggling act' of chores and trying to lead a 'normal life'.
- Worries and anxieties – about the future, the child's progress, what's best for the child, the needs of other children in the family, possible marital breakdown and the deterioration of relationships between other family members.

The overall result is physical/mental/emotional exhaustion. On top of all this there is also social isolation caused by the following:

- Embarrassment about the child's erratic, unpredictable and often anti-social behaviour in public and the fear of not being able to deal with it, which leads to families not undertaking activities outside the home.
- Attitudes of family, friends, the local community and society at large contribute to unease and anxiety as they perceive criticism of their parenting skills because the child does not obey social rules.
- Marginalisation – there is still a perceived stigma attached to being 'different', not being regarded as a 'normal' family, feeling stripped of their family status and denied the same emotional and social worth as other more typical families.

Consider how parents feel in these situations:

### CASE STUDIES

Sally is 10 years old. She is very pretty, bright and chatty. When she is on the bus with her mum and a rather obese woman gets on, she says 'Oh look at that fat lady. She must eat far too much.' Her mum tries to keep her quiet and distract her with a sweet.

Omar is 9 and is waiting with his dad at the bus stop. When a bunch of lads start swearing, scrawling graffiti and smoking, he marches over to them, tells them how naughty they are and that they will die if they keep smoking. His dad pulls him away and tells him not to talk to big boys like that, but his reaction is 'But it's true!'

Ben is 19 and really enjoys a meal in the pub with his mum and dad. On the way out he spots another family at a nearby table. A little girl

*(Continued)*

> *(Continued)*
>
> has turned her stool on its side to make it higher to sit on, but Ben
> knows stools should not be on their side and rushes over to 'fix' it.
> His dad grabs him before he gets to her, so he flings himself on the
> floor and starts screaming and head-banging against the wall and
> everyone in the pub turns to watch.

## Financial and time issues

Looking after a disabled child is expensive – laundry, bedding, clothing,
heating, transport and replacing broken items. Parental careers and jobs are
often affected, as they may end up working below their skills in order to
have a job with enough flexibility to accommodate the need for more time
for dealing with professionals, meetings, hospital visits, special diets and
equipment and therapy provision. This, in turn, has a negative impact on
future pensions. Arrangements that will allow the care of a disabled child
may have a detrimental impact on the family's lifestyle and housing may be
inadequate for their needs.

## The media and autism

Newspapers, television, radio, and film within the past 15 years or so have
strongly influenced the concepts of autism held by the wider population.
Unfortunately, the interpretation of autism projected by the media has
tended to focus on emotion and ultimately is dictated by what makes a
saleable story. The end result has been to give a populist view of autism, pre-
senting individual examples of autism leading to simplistic interpretations
that give unrealistic impressions of autism. The portrayal of people with
autism is often negative, using emotive terminology such as 'illness', 'suffer-
ing' and 'affliction' and encouraging parents to be constantly looking for a
'cure'.

   The first big global media portrayal of autism came with Dustin Hoffman's
role as Raymond in the 20th Century Fox film *Rainman*. For many in the UK
the description 'autistic savant' was first heard, as was the view that all
people with autism had spectacular abilities in highly unusual areas such as
recall of dates, events, and mathematical calculations that could be put to
good use for financial gain on the gambling tables of Las Vegas. As a piece of

cinema it made for good viewing but as a piece about autism it failed to provide a satisfactory and truthful view. But there again, it will never have set out to do so. Indeed, the media representation of autism has never sought to present the truth of autism but rather to sell for profit emotional interpretations of it.

In 1998 the debate over the combined vaccine for measles, mumps and rubella (MMR) kicked off with Dr Andrew Wakefield's contention of a link between the triple MMR vaccine and autism, and with this another emotional story relating to autism had arrived for the media to use. The MMR debate seemed to bring out the very worst in people, where attribution of blame and defence against these accusations became the prime public perception of autism. The public may have then heard about autism, but their view was coloured by a perception that autism was something entirely negative and mothers did not want their children to have it. The damage caused by the MMR debate upon public health has been far reaching.

In recent years there has been a proliferation of autobiographies of variable quality and even TV programmes and dramatisations giving more personal perspectives of living with autism. Again, these programmes tend to have strong personal and emotional hooks rather than just the focus on autism. The reality is that the media have never used the story of autism to be of genuine service to the autism community and indeed families with autism, but rather to serve their own ends.

What can we learn from this? Firstly, if, you are ever approached by the media to project your story, take stock and be wary. It is the media who will determine the outcome and spin to put on your story and their judgment will be based upon what they need to project and emphasise. Very recently a senior director of a national television station told one of the authors: 'Be under no illusion. The reporter who appears to want to be your best friend really just wants a story that can sell. Usually, he/she doesn't give a damn about individuals with autism, about families and about those who work with autism.'

### Dealing with the media

- Ask for questions in advance, with time to consider and prepare your responses.
- Do not answer questions outside those that you have prepared answers to and agreed to respond to.
- Try to control the interview and do not respond to questions repeatedly put in different ways by interviewers.

- Avoid putting your child in photographs – the repetitive use of photographs of the individual children strips them of their right to privacy and dignity. Ask yourself the question: do I want my child identified in this way?

## Summary

Taking all these issues into account, it is important that individual family members make time for themselves and do not allow autism to completely take over their lives. It is all too easy to become so sucked into the world of autism that everything else takes second place, but family members are far more likely to collapse (maybe even literally) under the strain if they do not guard against physical, mental and emotional breakdown.

Joining a support group and sharing your concerns with other people in a similar situation can be a real help. Other parents know where you are coming from because they have been there too and they can be a real source of emotional and practical support and information. It is reassuring to know others who are facing the same problems and those who may be ahead of you in the game because their child is older and has moved on to the stage that you will be approaching next. Some overbearing parents may be a little too ready to tell others what they feel they should be doing, but it is helpful to join together with other families to campaign for better services. Groups that organise family activities so that they can all have fun together are particularly useful – it doesn't all have to be talking about problems. Siblings can find other children there who have an 'odd' brother or sister like they do, so that can be a real support to them, and the autistic children will often find a playmate like themselves, which can be very satisfying, while the parents chat.

**REFLECTIVE OASIS**

How much time do you take as 'me' time each day, each week? If the answer is 'I don't, there is too much else to do', think about what will happen to your child with autism and to the rest of the family if you fall apart...

## Points to remember

- You do not have to be the perfect parent – nobody gets it right all the time and everybody needs rest and recreation
- Take every opportunity offered you for help and support – especially if it means you can take a break. Don't feel guilty about taking time to do something you enjoy. You can 'recharge your batteries' in this way and be much more use to your child with autism and your family and friends when you are feeling refreshed and alert than when you are tired, jaded and overwhelmed
- Beware of contact with the media and its motives in wanting your story
- Local parent support groups can be a vital lifeline of support and information

# 10

# Finding information, help and support

This final chapter focuses on some of the sources of help available to families living with autism. It is not a comprehensive list but will hopefully point you in the right direction for a range of information needs.

## Information at your fingertips – where to start

Today there are well over 200 charities in the United Kingdom working on behalf of people with autism and their families. Some excellent work is undertaken by smaller local groups and it is important to seek out these as well as the more obvious big players such as the national charities in Scotland, Wales, Northern Ireland and England. Indeed the national charities of the Celtic nations (Wales, Northern Ireland and Scotland) have formed a partnership to share information, knowledge and ideas between their countries. So the national bodies can be a good starting place for sources of information about family support, education and other services at local and national level. Here are some useful organisations known to the authors.

### Autism-specific organisations

National Autistic Society (*note*: The NAS is an English-based charity which also does some work in Wales, Scotland and Northern Ireland)

393 City Rd
London
EC1V 1NE

Tel. 020 7833 2299 for general enquiries
Helpline: 0845 070 4004
Parent to Parent support line: 0800 9 520 520
Email: **nas@nas.org.uk**
Website: **www.nas.org.uk**

Autism Northern Ireland (PAPA)
Donard
Knockbracken Healthcare Park
Saintfield
Belfast
BT8 8BH

Tel. 0208 9040 1729
Email: **info@autismni.org**
Website: **www.autismni.org**

The Scottish Society for Autism
Head Office
Hilton House
Alloa Business Park
Whins Rd
Alloa
FK10 3SA

Tel. 01259 720 044
Email: **autism@autism-in-scotland.org.uk**
Website: **www.autism-in-scotland.org.uk**

Autism Cymru (Wales' national charity for autism)
National Office
6 Great Darkgate St
Aberystwyth
Ceredigion
SY23 1DE

Tel. 01970 625 256
Email: **sue@autismcymru.org**
Website: **www.awares.org**

autism.west midlands (covers the whole West Midlands region)
18 Highfield Rd
Edgbaston
Birmingham
B15 3DU

Tel. 0121 450 7575 for the Information Service Helpline 10am–2pm
Email: **info@autismwestmidlands.org.uk**
Website: **www.autismwestmidlands.org.uk**

Autism Initiatives UK (a charity providing a range of services to adults with ASD throughout the UK and Isle of Man)
7 Chesterfield Rd
Crosby
Liverpool
L23 9XL

Tel. 0151 300 9500
Email: **headoffice@autisminitiatives.org**
Website: **www.autisminitiatives.org**

## Education

For free copies of *The Special Educational Needs Code of Practice* and the useful booklet *Special Educational Needs (SEN): A Guide for Parents and Carers,* contact:

The Publications Department
The Department for Education and Skills
PO Box 5050
Sherwood Park
Annesley
Nottingham
NG15 0DJ

Tel. 0845 602 2260
Email: **dfes@prolog.uk.com**
Website: **www.dfes.gov.uk/sen**

Since devolution there are different codes of practice in Scotland and Wales. Please contact:

The Scottish Executive
Victoria Quay
Edinburgh
EH6 3QQ

Tel. 0131 556 8400

The Education Department
National Assembly for Wales
Cathays Park
Cardiff
CF10 3NQ

Tel. 029 2082 6078

The Children's Legal Centre
University of Essex
Wivenhoe Park
Colchester
CO4 3FQ

An independent, national charity concerned with law and policy affecting children and young people. They operate an Education Law and Advocacy Unit and their lawyers and barristers provide free legal advice on all aspects of education law. Contact: 0845 120 2966 (charged at local rate) 10am–1pm.

SENDIST – for legal appeals and tribunals
Procession House
55 Ludgate Hill
London
EC4M 7JW

Tel. 020 7029 9726
SEN helpline: 0870 241 2555
Discrimination helpline: 0870 606 5750
Website: **www.sendist.gov.uk**

The Association of Specialist Colleges – for information on special needs colleges
NATSPEC Administrative Officer
36 Gresham Rd
East Ham

London
E6 6DS

Tel. and Fax: 020 8471 3284
Email: **janicefaldo.natspec@btinternet.com**
Website: **www.natspec.org.uk**

Camphill-run schools, colleges and communities
The Camphill Advisory Service
19 South Rd
Stourbridge
West Midlands
DY8 3YA

Tel. 01384 441 505
Website (England, Wales and Northern Ireland): **www.camphill.org.uk**
(Scotland): **www.camphillscotland.org.uk**

Advisory Centre for Education (ACE) offers advice and guidance on all aspects of state education
1c Aberdeen Studios
22–24 Highbury Grove
London
N5 2DQ

Helpline: 0808 800 5793
Website: **www.ace.ed.org.uk**

Education Otherwise provide support and information for families who want to home-educate their children
PO Box 7420
London
N9 9SG (enclose an A5 SAE)

Tel.   (England): 0870 7653 510
       (Scotland): 0870 7653 580
       (Ireland): 0870 7653 610
       (Wales): 0870 7653 620
       Website: **www.education-otherwise.org**

Independent Panel for Special Educational Advice (IPSEA) offers independent, free advice on the duties of local authorities with regard to the educational needs of children with SEN and produces a very useful booklet about going to tribunal called *Sent Ahead*

6 Carlow Mews
Woodbridge
Suffolk
IP12 1EA

Advice Line (England and Wales): 0800 018 4016
(Scotland): 0131 454 0082
(Northern Ireland): 01232 705 654
Website: **www.ipsea.org.uk**

Centre for Studies on Inclusive Education (CSIE) – for information and advice on educating children with SEN in mainstream schools

New Redland
Frenchay Campus
Coldharbour Lane
Bristol
BS16 1QU

Tel. 0117 344 4007
Fax: 0117 344 4005
Website: **http://inclusion.uwe.ac.uk/csie**

National Association for Special Educational Needs (NASEN) – offers publications, training and research to promote development of SEN
4/5 Amber Business Village
Amber Close
Amington
Tamworth
Staffordshire
B77 4RP

Tel. 01827 311 500
Website: **www.nasen.org.uk**

National Portage Association – provides home learning schemes for pre-school children
PO Box 3075
Yeovil
BA21 3FB

Tel. and Fax: 01905 471 641
Email: **npa@portageuk.freeserve.co.uk**
Website: **www.portage.org.uk**

Network 81 – for information and guidance around SEN provision
1-7 Woodfield Terrace
Stanstead
Essex
CM24 8AJ

Tel. 0870 770 3262
Helpline: 0870 770 3306 (Mon–Fri 10am–2pm)
Email: **network81@tesco.net**
Website: **www.network81.co.uk**

Parents For Inclusion – for the right of children with disabilities to attend mainstream schools
Unit 2 Ground Floor
70 South Lambeth
London
SW8 1RL

Tel. 020 7735 7735
Email: **info@parentsforinclusion.org**
Website: **www.parentsforinclusion.org**

Pre-school Learning Alliance – for playgroups for under-5's

Email: **pla@pre-school.org.uk**
Website: **www.pre-school.org**

Rathbone Society – runs a helpline for children with disabilities and pro-duces a very helpful guide, *Making a Statement*
4th Floor
56 Oxford St
Manchester
M1 6EU

Tel. 0800 917 6790
Asian Language Line: 020 0800 085 4528
Email: **advice@rathbonetraining.co.uk**
Website: **www.rathbonetraining.co.uk**

Connexions – supports all young people aged 13–19 (and up to 25 if they have a disability or SEN). Personal advisors provide information on education, employment and personal issues. All areas of England have a Connexions Service. Ring 080 800 13 2 19 or visit the website: **www.connexions. gov.uk** for a local contact.

Parents' Autism Campaign for Education (PACE) – helps parents access specialist and appropriate education for children with autism
PACE
1 Floral Place
off Northampton Grove
London
N1 2FS

Tel. 020 7226 5525
Email: **info@pace-uk.org**
Website: **www.pace-uk.org**

### Financial

Disability Alliance – campaigns for disabled people and their families and can offer benefits entitlement advice
Universal House
88–94 Wentworth St
London
E1 7SA

Tel. 020 7247 8776
Fax: 020 7247 8765
Website: **www.disabilityalliance.org**

Disability Benefit Enquiry Line – for benefits advice
Freephone 0800 882 200

Disability Living Allowance Advice Line

Tel. 08457 123 456 (local rate)

Disability Information Advice Line (DIAL) – for help and advice on getting benefits and allowances: DIAL UK (Doncaster)

Tel. 01302 310 123

The Family Fund (Joseph Rowntree Foundation) – government funded to provide (means-tested) grants to families caring for severely disabled children under the age of 16 for items such as washing machines, bedding, clothing, driving lessons for carers, outings and holidays

PO Box 50
York
YO1 2ZX

For information on direct payments:

National Centre for Independent Living
250 Kennington Lane
London
SE11 5RD

Tel. 020 7587 1663

The Shaw Trust
Shaw House
Epsom Square
Whitehorse Business Park
Trowbridge
Wiltshire
BA14 0XJ

Tel. 01225 716 300
Website: **www.shaw-trust.org.uk**

## Communication

AFASIC (Association for all Speech Impaired Children)
2nd Floor
50–52 Great Sutton St
London
EC1V ODJ

Helpline: 0845 3 55 55 77 (local rate)
Fax: 020 7251 2834
Email: **info@afasic.org.uk**
Website: **www.afasic.org.uk**

I CAN – help and support for children with speech and language difficulties
and their families
4 Dyers Buildings
Holborn
London
EC1N 2QP

Tel. 0845 225 4071
Fax: 0845 225 4072
Website: **www.ican.org.uk**

Association of Speech and Language Therapists in Independent Practice –
can provide information on speech and language therapists who offer an
independent service to children with ASD

ASLTIP
Coleheath Bottom
Speen
Princes Risborough
Bucks ·
HP27 OSZ

Tel. 0870 241 3357 (answerphone)
Fax: 01494 488 590
Email: **asltip@awdry.demon.co.uk**
Website: **www.asltip.co.uk**

### Leisure and holidays

The National Autistic Society is one source of information about organisations that offer holidays for families living with autism.

Kidsactive is a national information service on all aspects of play
Pryor's Bank
Bishop's Park
London
SW6 3LA

Tel. 020 7736 4443
Helpline: 020 7731 1435

Email: **ntis@kidsactive.org.uk**
Website: **www.kidsactive.org.uk**

Write Away – a penfriend club for young people with SEN
1 Thorpe Close
London
W10 5XL

Tel. 020 8964 4225

Kids'Clubs Network – information for parents, schools and employers
Bellerive House

3 Muirfield Crescent
London
E14 9SZ

Tel. 020 7512 2112
Helpline: 020 7512 2100
Email: **information.office@kidsclubs.org.uk**
Website: **www.kidsclubs.org.uk**

National Association of Toy and Leisure Libraries
68 Churchway
London
NW1 1LT

Tel. 020 7387 9592
Email: **admin@natll.org.uk**
Website: **www.natll.org.uk**

Abilitynet – for information about computers and software for children with
special needs

PO Box 94
Warwick
CV34 5WS

Tel. 01926 312 847
Email: **enquiries@abilitynet.co.uk**
Website: **www.abilitynet.co.uk**

Disabled Living Foundation – information on new technologies, equipment and training methods for people with disabilities
380–384 Harrow Rd
London
W9 2HU

Tel. 020 7289 6111
Helpline: 0845 130 9177
Website: **www.dlf.org.uk**

Fledglings – a free search service for resources for children with SEN, especially unusual items not readily available
6 Southfield
Ickleton
Saffron Walden
CB10 1TE

Tel. 0845 458 1124
Fax: 0845 458 1125
Email: **enquiries@fledglings.org.uk**
Website: **www.fledglings.org.uk**

### Legal services

Community Legal Service – provides information about legal rights and a directory of solicitors and advisors on specific topics.
Website: **www.justask. com**

Disability Rights Commission – provides information on the Disability Discrimination Act
DRC
FREEPOST MID 02164
Stratford-upon-Avon
CV37 9BR

Tel. 08457 622 633
Email: **enquiry@drc-gb.org**
Website: **www.drc.gb.org**

Disability Law Service – free legal representation and advice for people with disabilities

39–45 Cavell St
London
E1 2BP

Tel. 020 7791 9800
Fax: 020 7791 9802
Website: **www.mkurrein.co.uk**

### *General*

Mencap provides learning disability related information and produces a very useful booklet on wills and leaving money to a relative with a learning disability
123 Golden Lane
London
EC1Y ORT

Tel. 020 7696 0454
Fax: 020 7696 5540
Email: **information@mencap.org.uk**
Website: **www.mencap.org.uk**

BILD (British Institute of Learning Disability)
Campion House
Green St
Kidderminster
Worcestershire
DY10 1JL

Tel. 01562 723 010
Website: **www.bild.org.uk**

Contact a Family – provides information on all aspects of caring for a child with a disability or special need and produces some very helpful publications
209–211 City Rd
London
EC1V 1JN

Tel. 020 7608 8700
Fax: 020 7608 8701
Minicom: 020 7608 8702

Email: **info@cafamily.org.uk**
Website: **www.cafamily.org.uk**

Council for Disabled Children – information on all issues relating to children and disability, especially Parent Partnership Services and Children's Disability Registers
National Children's Bureau
London
WC1V 7QE

Tel. 020 7843 6000
Fax: 020 7278 9512
Website: **www.ncb.org.uk**

OAASIS (Office for Advice, Assistance, Support and Information on Special Needs) – provides a wealth of disability related information, including very useful factsheets on autism and related conditions
Brock House
Grigg Lane
Brockenhurst
Hampshire
SO42 7RE

Helpline: 09068 633 201
Fax: 01590 622 687
Email: **oasis@hesleygroup.co.uk**
Website: **www.oaasis.co.uk**

RADAR – campaigns and provides information on disability issues. Radar keys unlock public toilets for the disabled and are a boon for parents out and about with an autistic child of the opposite gender from themselves
12 City Forum
250 City Rd
London
EC1V 8AF

Tel. 020 7250 3222
Fax: 020 7250 0212
Minicom: 020 7250 4119

Email: **radar@radar.org.uk**
Website: **www.radar.org.uk**

### Other

The British Psychological Society – has a list of independent educational psychologists
St Andrews House
48 Princess Road East
Leicester
LE1 7DR

Tel. 0116 254 9568
Fax: 0116 247 0787
Email: **enquiry@bps.org.uk**
Website: **www.bps.org.uk**

Eagle House – for psychological, speech and language and occupational therapy assessments
224 London Rd
Mitcham
Surrey
CR4 3HD

Tel. 020 8687 7050
Fax: 020 8687 7055
Email: **admin@eaglehouseschool.co.uk**

### The internet

The internet holds an enormous range of material on autistic spectrum disorders but, as we all know, the internet has its dangers as well, and the case of autism is no different; there are many, many dubious sites. The key to starting to use the internet to discover more about autistic spectrum disorders is by visiting authoritative national sites as the first port of call, which can then lead onto links for other helpful sites and resources.

**Finding out about local resources from authoritative internet sites**

Scotland: **www.autism-in-scotland.org.uk** (run by the Scottish Society for Autism); and **www.scottishautismnetwork.org.uk** (run by Strathclyde University)

Northern Ireland: **www.autismni.org** (run by Autism Northern Ireland – PAPA)

Wales: **www.awares.org** (a bi-lingual site for Wales run by Autism Cymru – the Welsh national charity for autism)

England: **www.nas.org.uk** (a UK site run by the National Autistic Society)

Other key sites for information include

OAASIS: **www.oaasis.co.uk** (the office for advice, assistance, support and information on special needs)

Autismconnect: **www.autismconnect.org** (the world wide portal for autism)

**www.thearc.org/siblingsupport** Offers two sites: SibKids (for younger brothers and sisters) and SibNet (for older siblings)

**www.asperger.org**

**www.autismawareness.org.uk**

**www.autism-resources.com**

**www.autismuk.com**

**www.autistic.net**

**www.lookingupautism.org**

**www.mental-health-matters.com**

**www.youngminds.org.uk**

# References

Bleach, F. (2001) *Everybody is Different: A Book for Young People Who Have Brothers or Sisters with Autism.* London: NAS Publications

Bogdashina, O. (2006) *Theory of Mind and the Triad of Perspectives on Autism and Asperger Syndrome – A View From the Bridge.* London: Jessica Kingsley Publishers

Caldwell, P. (2003) *Crossing the Minefield: Establishing Safe Passage Through the Sensory Chaos of Autistic Spectrum Disorder.* Brighton: Pavilion

Carpenter, B. (2000) Sustaining the family: Meeting the needs of families of children with disabilities. *British Journal of Special Education,* 27 (3), 135–144

Carpenter, B. and Egerton, J. (eds) (2005) *Early Childhood Intervention: International Perspectives, National Initiatives and Regional Practice.* Coventry: West Midlands SEN Regional Partnership

Corea, I. (2003) BME communities – Autism and Asperger syndrome. **http://autism-ethnic-uk.tripod.com.**

Coulter, R. (2006) The Northern Ireland Autism Act. A Presentation held in The Northern Ireland Assembly, Stormont, Belfast, 21 June 2006.

Crissey, P. (2005) *Personal Hygiene: What's That Got to Do With Me?* London: Jessica Kingsley Publishers

Davies, J. (1995a) *Able Autistic Children: A Booklet for Brothers and Sisters.* Nottingham: Early Years Diagnostic Centre

Davies, J. (1995b) *Children with Autism: A Booklet for Brothers and Sisters.* Nottingham: Early Years Diagnostic Centre

DfES (2001) *Special Educational Needs (SEN): A Guide for Parents and Carers.* Nottingham: DfES Publications

DfES (2002) *Autistic Spectrum Disorders: Good Practice Guidance.* Nottingham: DfES Publications

DfES (2004) *Code of Practice on the Identification and Assessment of Special Educational Needs.* Nottingham: DfES Publications

DoH (2004) *Every Child Matters.* London: Department of Health Publications

Gorman, J.C. (2004) *Working With Challenging Parents.* California: Corwin Press

Gorrod, L. (1997) *My Brother is Different: A Book for Young Children Who Have Brothers and Sisters with Autism.* London: NAS Publications

Haddon, M. (2003) *The Curious Incident of the Dog in the Night Time.* Oxford: David Fickling Books

Hannah, L. (2001) *Teaching Young Children with Autistic Spectrum Disorders to Learn – A Practical Guide For Parents and Staff in Mainstream Schools and Nurseries.* London: NAS Publications

Henwood, M. (2003) Autism: Time for an autism strategy? *Community Care,* 31 January 2003.

Hoopman, K. (2000) *Blue Bottle Mystery.* London: Jessica Kingsley Publishers

Hoopman, K. (2001) *Of Mice and Aliens.* London: Jessica Kingsley Publishers

IPSEA (2002) *Sent Ahead.* Woodbridge, Suffolk: Independent Panel for Special Educational Advice

Jackson, L. (2003) *Freaks, Geeks and Asperger Syndrome.* London: Jessica Kingsley Publishers

Jones, G., Jordan, R. and Morgan, H. (2001) *All About Autistic Spectrum Disorders – An Information Guide for Parents and Carers.* London: Foundation for People with Learning Disabilities

Morgan, H. (2000) *Adults with Autism: A Guide to Theory and Practice.* Cambridge: Cambridge University Press

NAS Autism Helpline (1999) *What is Asperger Syndrome and How Will it Affect Me?* London: NAS Publications

NAS (2001) *Approaches to Autism.* London: NAS Publications

NAS (2003) *National Autism Plan for Children.* Royal College of Paediatrics and Child Health; Royal College of Psychiatrists. London: NAS

NAS (2006) *How Do You Feel Thomas?* London: Egmont UK Limited

Nind, M. and Hewett, D. (2001) *A Practical Guide to Intensive Interaction.* Kidderminster: BILD

Randall, P. and Parker, J. (1999) *Supporting the Families of Children with Autism.* Chichester: Wiley

Row, S. (2005) *Surviving the Special Educational Needs System: How to be a Velvet Bulldozer.* London: Jessica Kingsley Publishers

Royal College of Psychiatrists (2006) *Psychiatric Services for Adolescents and Adults with Asperger Syndrome and Other Autistic Spectrum Disorders.* London: The Royal College of Psychiatrists

Sainsbury, C. (2000) *Martian in the Playground.* Bristol: Lucky Duck Publishing

Scott, L. and Kerr-Edwards, L. (2003) *Talking Together … About Sex and Relationships.* London: fpa

Scott, L. and Kerr-Edwards, L. (2004) *Talking Together … About Growing Up.* London: fpa

Scottish Executive (2001) *The Public Health Institute Autistic Spectrum Disorder Needs Assessment Report.* Edinburgh: Scottish Executive

Segar, M. (1997) *Coping: A Survival Guide for People with Asperger Syndrome.* Nottingham: Early Years Diagnostic Centre

Vermeulen, P. (2000) *I Am Special: Introducing Children and Young People to their Autistic Spectrum Disorder.* London: Jessica Kingsley Publishers

Walker-Jones, E. (2005) *My Brother Gwern.* Aberystwyth: Autism Cymru Publications

Whitaker, P. (2001) *Challenging Behaviour and Autism – Making Sense, Making Progress – A Guide to Preventing and Managing Challenging Behaviour for Parents and Teachers.* London: NAS Publications

Wrobel, M. (2003) *Taking Care of Myself – A Healthy Hygiene, Puberty and Personal Curriculum for Young People with Autism.* Texas: Future Horizons

# Glossary

| | |
|---|---|
| **ADHD** | Attention Deficit Hyperactivity Disorder |
| **APPGA** | All Party Parliamentary Group for Autism |
| **AS** | Asperger Syndrome |
| **ASD** | Autistic Spectrum Disorder |
| **Autism Cymru** | Wales' national charity for autism |
| **BILD** | British Institute of Learning Disabilities |
| **CAMHS** | Child and Adolescent Mental Health Services |
| **CJS** | Criminal Justice System |
| **DfES** | Department for Education and Skills (England) |
| **DoH** | Department of Health |
| **DSM IV** | *Diagnostic and Statistical Manual* (Edition 4) |
| **EEG** | Electroencephalogram |
| **GAP** | *Good Autism Practice* – a journal published by BILD |
| **ICD 10** | International Classification of Diseases |
| **IPSEA** | Independent Panel for Special Educational Advice |
| **LA** | Local Authority |

**LEA**                              Local Education Authority

**Mencap**                           The National Association for Mentally Handicapped
                                     People

**NAP-C**                            National Autism Plan for Children

**NAS**                              National Autistic Society

**PECS**                             Picture Exchange Communication System

**PPS**                              Parent Partnership Services

**SENCo**                            Special Educational Needs Co-ordinator

**SENDIST**                          Special Educational Needs and Disability Tribunal

**Social Stories**                   A strategy developed by Carol Gray to teach indi-
                                     viduals with ASD appropriate social skills

**TEACCH**                           Treatment and Education of Autistic and Related
                                     Communication Handicapped Children

**Triad of Impairments**             Difficulties encountered by individuals with ASD
                                     in social understanding, social communication
                                     and rigidity of thought first referred to by Lorna
                                     Wing and Judy Gould in 1979

# Index